THE **REALLY, REALLY, REALLY EAS**

STEP-BY-STEP GUIDE TO

ONLINE BUYING & SELLING

for absolute beginners of all ages

Gavin Hoole and Cheryl Smith

Contents

Read this before you start

ONLINE BUYING AND SELLING ARE BOTH FUN AND EASY!

Every day more and more people are buying and selling goods and services via the Internet. eBay has become a household name and is the world's largest online auctions site, with over 200,000,000 members, and 100,000,000 items to choose from on any given day. Likewise, Amazon.com is well known as the world's largest online store and craigslist is the undisputed 'biggie' when it comes to online classified advertising, with 9 billion page views per day.

   This book will help you to get on board too and enjoy the many benefits of using this relatively new means of convenient trading from the comfort of your own home. Welcome to the world of online buying and selling!

YOUR ONLINE JOURNEY WITH THIS STEP-BY-STEP BOOK

Assuming one is already somewhat Internet-savvy, probably the biggest stumbling block to getting started with online trading is the concerns people have about Internet fraud and making payments online, especially when using a credit card. This book will help you to see that it's not as scary as many people make it out to be. There are a few safety measures you can take to minimize the risk.

   Our journey starts with an explanation of the various payment options available and it takes you along the following course:

1 **Payment methods:** We'll get this out of the way right upfront. What you learn in this chapter will apply to all online buying and selling in the chapters that follow.

2 **Making a straightforward online purchase:** Here you will learn how to search for an item at an online store, add it to your 'shopping basket', proceed through the virtual checkout, pay for it and get it delivered to you by mail.

3 **Buying at online auctions:** Here is where you'll extend that knowledge and learn how to buy at an online auction, where you'll be bidding for the item of your choice in much the same way as offline auctions work at auction houses in your own town or city.

4 **Selling at online auctions:** Stretching your knowledge further, you will learn the essential ins and outs of selling something at an online auction and getting paid by your customer.

5 **Exploring other online buying and selling options:** Here we'll introduce you to other possibilities that you can explore, such as buying and selling at online stores and auction sites in your own country, and making use of online classifieds to buy and sell within your local area.

 WORK YOUR WAY THROUGH EACH CHAPTER IN SEQUENCE This step-by-step workbook is designed to be used chapter by chapter. Working through it in its proper sequence will help you do 'first things first' and become familiar with the various terms and procedures. Each chapter serves as a stepping-stone to the next.

THE USER-FRIENDLY VISUAL SYSTEM

The same user-friendly visual system as used in all the books in this series makes it really, really, really easy for you to enjoy your first experience of online buying and selling.

Colour-coded text windows are used so that you can see at a glance the *type* of information you're looking at:

- introductions and explanations in normal black text on a white background;

- step-by-step action procedures in yellow boxes;

- hints and tips in blue boxes;

- very important notes and warnings in boxes with red borders;

- supportive explanatory information in grey panels.

Where necessary, the detailed procedures are supported by screenshots of actual Web page windows to make learning easier. In fact, screenshots abound in this book.

 WEB PAGES ARE DYNAMIC AND ALWAYS CHANGING Companies like Amazon.com and eBay have websites in several countries, and their Web page layouts can differ from country to country. In addition, Web pages themselves are constantly being revamped as new features or systems are added to the service. On top of all of that, the actual page *content* changes daily as new items become available for sale or auction. So use the screenshots in this book as a guide. If the page you see on your computer screen looks quite different, simply use the principles given in the book and make your own adaptations as necessary.

INVITATION: VISIT THIS BOOK'S COMPANION WEBSITE

If you need help with using a computer, accessing the Internet, or finding out something more about online buying or selling, you're invited to visit our companion website. There you'll find details of our range of **Really, Really, Really Easy books** covering a variety of subjects for absolute beginners – e.g. **computers, digital photography, creating your family tree, building your own website** and, of course, **online buying and selling**. From our website you can also access our **discussion forums** where you can ask questions and even help other 'newbie's'. Our website URL is:

<u>http://www.ReallyEasyComputerBooks.com</u>

Let's have some fun!

1 Payment methods

THE PAYMENT AND SECURITY DILEMMA

The main concern that most beginners have when it comes to buying something online, is how to be sure that no one can defraud them of their money by misusing their credit card or banking details.

So, before we even start getting into the steps of buying and selling online let's first deal with the last stage: making the payment. Once you understand the various methods and safeguards available, you can select the options that best suit you and apply those to your future online transactions.

Some typical concerns

- I have a credit card, but I'm afraid of giving my card details out on the Internet.
- What if my credit card details find their way into the hands of some unscrupulous website operator, or even a hacker?
- What if I buy something and I don't receive what I've bought, but the seller has already debited my credit card?
- I don't have a credit card and am not able to get one (e.g. blacklisted due to bad credit ratings in the past).
- I don't have a bank account or a credit card.

We'll deal with most of these concerns now. Non-receipt of goods you've bought online is an issue we'll deal with in a later chapter.

PAYMENT BY CREDIT CARD

Using a credit card is one of the quickest and most popular ways of paying for purchases online, and one that we ourselves have used for many years without any problems at all. If there's a debit on your credit card account that you believe is wrong, you can query it with your credit card company and, if you did not authorize it, you can dispute it and ask them to reverse it.

NOTE: CHECK YOUR COUNTRY'S FOREIGN EXCHANGE RULES

Some countries may restrict the use of a credit card for international payments. If you're unsure about your country's rules, check with your bank or credit card company.

Here's how a typical online credit card payment works:
- When you are ready to finalize your purchase and authorize the supplier to debit your credit card account, a window will appear on your screen asking for your details.

• The standard information you'll be asked for is the following, though not necessarily in this sequence:

Your name	Exactly as it appears on your credit card
Credit card type	E.g. VISA, MasterCard, American Express
Card number	The 16-digit number on the front of the card – e.g. 4901 XXXX 7777 9999
The CVV verification number	The 3- or 4-digit number on the reverse side of your card, to the right of the card number – or printed on the front of American Express cards. (Some cards show only the last four digits of the 16-digit card number on the back of the card; the 3-digit CVV number will appear after those 4 digits.)

3-digit CVV code on the back of a typical card

4-digit CVV code on front of an American Express card

WHAT IS A CVV NUMBER?

When you use your credit card to pay at your local store, you are required to sign the voucher or key in a personal ID number so that the checkout person can verify that you are indeed the owner of the card, by comparing your voucher signature with that on the back of the credit card or by verifying the number. With online transactions this is obviously not possible. This means that if someone happens to know your name and credit card number, they could try to effect a transaction on your account without your knowledge. The CVV number takes the place, in a way, of your written signature or pin code authorization. It is an additional attempt to reduce potential fraud. Only the person who holds the actual card in their hand should know this number. So, by entering the CVV number in the online payment form you are, in effect, confirming your right to use that credit card to make the payment, because you have the physical card with you.

Various credit card companies use different terms to refer to this number, such as CVV2 (Card Verification Value), CVC2 (Card Validation Code), CID (Card Identification), etc. But they all refer to the same 3- or 4-digit number on the reverse or front of credit cards. Note that the CVV number is not part of the credit card account number itself.

TIP: CHECK WHETHER THE WEBSITE IS SECURE

As additional protection, make sure that the Web page asking for your payment details indicates that your data is protected by Secure Socket Layer (SSL) technology. You'll know it is if the URL (page address) has an 's' after the standard http – e.g. https://www.paypal.com

WHAT IS SSL TECHNOLOGY?

Ordinary Web pages have an address (URL) that starts with *http* (e.g. http://www.amazon.com). These pages do not need to have such security in place. A page that has SSL technology, such as a sign-up or login page, will have a URL that has an 's' at the end of the *http* to indicate that it is a secure site when it comes to sensitive data transmission – e.g. Amazon.com's sign-up page: https://www.amazon.com/gp/sign-in.html

DON'T BE CONNED BY 'SECURITY' IMAGES ON WEB PAGES Unfortunately there *are* some con-artists who are operating websites out there, and their Web pages can sometimes look very convincing. So if you see the 🔒 lock icon on a Web page, it may just be a *picture* and not a true indication that the site is protected by SSL technology. Likewise, the well-known VeriSign logo (see below) may also just be a JPEG image that's been lifted off a truly secure Web page with the intention of fooling an unsuspecting visitor that the site is secure and that any personal data will be secure when it is submitted.

Anyone can save an image – like one of the VeriSign icons, or a security padlock similar to those shown here – from a secure website and then add it to their own Web pages to create the impression that their site is secure.

How to test the validity of security icons

Note that the security padlock icon should appear in the website's *address bar* and/or in the *status bar* at the bottom of your browser (Internet Explorer, Firefox, Safari, Opera, etc.) and *not* in the web page window itself.

1 Click on the 🔒 **lock icon** (or the VeriSign or other security icon) to open the website's SSL Certificate which should display the following details:
  • Domain name
  • Company name and address, with city and country
  • Certificate expiry date
  • Name of the Certification Authority that issued the certificate

2 If you do not see this kind of information, then treat the so-called secure site with a degree of mistrust, and make your decision accordingly.

NOTE: YOUR BROWSER SHOULD GIVE YOU A WARNING

When a browser connects to a secure site it will retrieve the site's SSL Certificate and check that it has not expired, that it has been issued by a genuine Certification Authority which the browser trusts, and that it is being used by the website for which it has been issued. If the site fails on any one of these checks, the browser will display a warning.

Credit card advantages:

- Quick and easy, with immediate authorization and prompt shipment of your order or access to download the digital document or software you've paid for;
- No fees, interest or extra charges, provided you pay your credit card balance in full by the due date;
- Fraud protection by your credit card company, where you can dispute any incorrect debits and be refunded if applicable (e.g. charges you did not authorize; wrong amount debited versus price advertised).

Fears/concerns:

- You may worry that your credit card details are now 'out there' and vulnerable to abuse.
- You may find it difficult to control your credit card spending, so feel that using a credit card does not suit your particular needs.

Suggested solutions:

- Get a separate credit card for Internet transactions only, and ask the credit card company to set the credit limit to a much lower level than you would have on a normal credit card.
- Order a *prepaid* credit card or a *virtual* credit card online, whereby you pay money into the card account to be used for online payments. (See further on in this chapter for an explanation of these options.)
- Register with eBay's trusted and secure PayPal system that protects all your confidential credit card and banking details from other parties, such as sellers (see next topic).

PAYMENT VIA PAYPAL

PayPal is a highly respected intermediary payment processing service owned by eBay, and is the only online payment system that is fully integrated with eBay's online trading systems.

PayPal offers a very secure and quick method of making online payments or transferring funds to family and friends, if they too have a PayPal account. PayPal can be used not only at eBay but also at many other online trading sites and reputable online stores, wherever the PayPal payment option is displayed. To register with PayPal (registration is free) you'll need the following:

- a valid email address, and
- either a valid credit card, or
- a valid bank account in one of the over fifty countries specified on PayPal's website.

PayPal's corporate headquarters at eBay's satellite office campus in San Jose, California

How PayPal works

- When you're ready to pay for a purchase, you:
  - select the option to pay via PayPal;
  - log in to your PayPal account, fill in the required data and follow the prompts.
- PayPal then transfers the money immediately to the seller and within two business days it debits the primary account you nominated in your PayPal account settings (either your credit card or your bank account – if your bank account is in one of the countries in which PayPal offers this option).

Some advantages of PayPal

- *Fast:* As with credit card payments, PayPal payments are electronic and therefore much faster than waiting for bank drafts or money orders to arrive, or cheques to be cleared by the bank.
- *Secure:* PayPal assures us that it uses the highest commercially-available encryption technology to protect your data.
- *Private:* PayPal holds your information securely and does not disclose it to anyone else, not even the person being paid. So, by using PayPal you can pay people online without ever divulging your card or bank account details to them.
- *Free payments:* PayPal does not charge you any fees when you pay a supplier or send money to someone online.
- *Buyer protection:* PayPal's Buyer Complaint Policy covers you in the event of any incorrect charges or an item you paid for but did not receive. (Your claim must be filed within 45 days of payment.)
- *Global:* PayPal operates worldwide and is accepted in many countries, some of which have their own PayPal websites.
- *Online transaction records:* By logging in at the PayPal website with your secure user name and password, you can access a complete record of your PayPal transactions.
- *Ideal for sellers too:* Sellers can accept payment from customers using a credit card, even though the seller does not have his/her own credit card processing facilities. PayPal charges the customer's credit card with the value of the service and transfers the money into the seller's PayPal account or specified bank account. This is great for individuals and small businesses that want to do online selling.

Concerns/disadvantages with PayPal

- In a number of countries, PayPal does not yet offer the facility of paying the buyer's funds into the seller's bank account. In such countries a seller must make alternative banking arrangements. You could consider opening an offshore bank account in one of the countries where PayPal does offer this facility (if feasible), or possibly try another payment service such as AlertPay. Their secure website is **www.alertpay.com**

To find PayPal's list of facilities by country:

1 Go to the PayPal Web page at **www.PayPal.com/worldwide**
2 Look in the various listings to find your own country and see what PayPal facilities are available to you.

Sample extracts from the PayPal Web page:

PayPal Localized Sites - Your Customized Total Payment Solution

Australia	France	Spain
Austria	Germany	Switzerland
Belgium	Italy	United Kingdom
Canada	Netherlands	United States
China	Poland	

Send. Receive. Withdraw.

Send. Receive. Withdraw to a Local or U.S. Bank Account or a card.
Send and receive payments in these countries. Withdraw from your PayPal account to your in-country bank account or to a U.S. bank account. In addition, withdraw to a credit, debit, or prepaid card in countries marked with a (†).

Czech Republic	Indonesia†	Portugal
Denmark	Ireland	Reunion
Finland	Japan	Singapore
French Guiana	Luxembourg†	Slovakia†

Send Money to Anyone in the Growing PayPal Network

Albania	Gabon Republic	Peru
Algeria	Gambia	Pitcairn Islands
Andorra	Greenland	Qatar
Angola	Grenada	Republic of the Congo
Anguilla	Guatemala	Russia
Antigua and Barbuda	Guinea	Rwanda

PAYMENT BY BANK DEBIT CARD

If you have a bank debit card with the VISA or MasterCard logo on it, you can use that as a means of payment too – either paying the merchant directly or paying via PayPal as the secure and privacy-protecting intermediary. Check with your bank, though, to make sure that this is possible for your country. We know, for example, that at the time of writing this book, international payments from South Africa cannot be made using a bank account's debit card, although credit card payments are quite acceptable in that country.

Notes about debit cards (where this option is available)

- If you don't have a credit card, but you do have a bank account, this method can be very useful because you cannot run up a huge debt like you can with a credit card. Your purchase will only be authorized if you have sufficient funds available in your bank account.
- If you're concerned that the vendor may gain access to *all* the money in your bank account through the debit card payment method, you could do one of two things:
  - Open a separate bank account (e.g. a savings account) with a debit card connected to it, and deposit only enough money in it to pay for your upcoming Internet purchases. Or, whenever you want to make an Internet payment, use your online banking facility to transfer enough funds from your main bank account into this special account, and then use the debit card linked to that special account to pay for your online purchase.
  - Alternatively, and provided your country allows online payments via a debit card, just pay through PayPal using your debit card – perhaps using the first option of the dedicated account too.

SETTING UP A PAYPAL ACCOUNT

Because PayPal is such a secure and popular worldwide alternative to making credit card payments directly to the seller, we'll take you through the sign-up process so that you have this system in place for your first purchase – assuming that you'd prefer to use PayPal instead of paying a private individual supplier directly with your credit card. (Incidentally, we ourselves have no concerns about paying directly by credit card to well-established companies such as Amazon.com and many of the other 'biggies'. Our main concern would be payments to unknown websites or private individuals.)

Localized country-specific websites

If you live in one of the following countries, you can register with PayPal through the local PayPal website:

Australia:	**https://www.paypal.com/au**		Italy:	**https://www.paypal.com/it**
Austria:	**https://www.paypal.com/at**		Netherlands:	**https://www.paypal.com/nl**
Belgium:	**https://www.paypal.com/be**		Poland:	**https://www.paypal.com/pl**
China:	**https://www.paypal.com/cn**		Spain:	**https://www.paypal.com/es**
Germany:	**https://www.paypal.com/de**		Switzerland:	**https://www.paypal.com/ch**
France:	**https://www.paypal.com/fr**		United Kingdom:	**https://www.paypal.com/uk**
Ireland:	**https://www.paypal.com/ie**			

NOTE: THE SEQUENCE MAY DIFFER FROM COUNTRY TO COUNTRY

The steps that follow are according to the current registration sequence we've used, starting at PayPal's international site in the US and selecting the United Kingdom as the country of registration. If you register in a different country, then you may need to adapt as necessary as you work through this tutorial.

1 Connect to the Internet and go to the international website at **www.PayPal.com** (can be all lower case, if you prefer).

2 Click on the **Sign Up** link at the top of the page.

3 In the **Choose Account Type** window, click on the ⌄ **down** arrows to select your country and language preferences from the drop-down lists.

4 Once you've selected your language preference and clicked on your country's name in the drop-down list, wait a few seconds for your country-specific page to load (you'll see your selected country displayed near the bottom of that page).

5 Read the descriptions of each account type; to see the fee structures for Premier and Business accounts, click on the **low fees** links.

6 To see a neat table showing the latest features of all three account types (second screenshot example below), click on the link **Learn more** at the end of the explanations.

7 When you've made your decision, click in the radio button next to the account you wish to register for (we've chosen the **Personal Account**); then click on **Continue**.

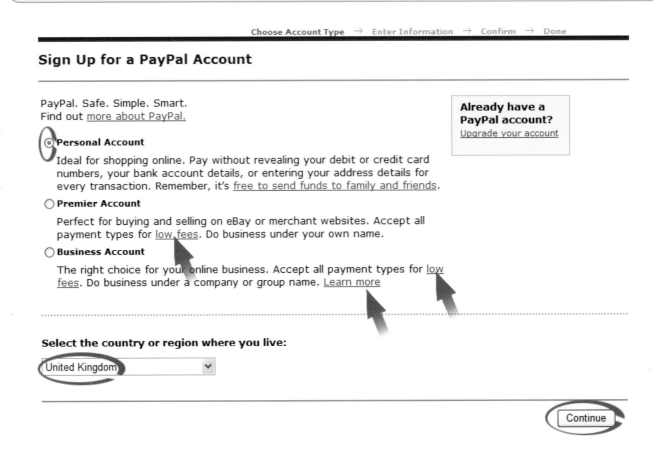

Choose Account Type → Enter Information → Confirm → Done

Sign Up for a PayPal Account

PayPal. Safe. Simple. Smart.
Find out more about PayPal.

Already have a PayPal account?
Upgrade your account

Personal Account
Ideal for shopping online. Pay without revealing your debit or credit card numbers, your bank account details, or entering your address details for every transaction. Remember, it's free to send funds to family and friends.

Premier Account
Perfect for buying and selling on eBay or merchant websites. Accept all payment types for low fees. Do business under your own name.

Business Account
The right choice for your online business. Accept all payment types for low fees. Do business under a company or group name. Learn more

Select the country or region where you live:

United Kingdom

Continue

Compare PayPal Account Types

Account Benefits	Personal	Premier	Business
Send money	✓	✓	✓
24-hour fraud surveillance	✓	✓	✓
Customer Service availability	✓	✓	✓
eBay Tools	Limited	✓	✓
Merchant Services	Limited	✓	✓
Accept credit or debit cards	Limited	✓	✓
PayPal Debit Card		✓	✓
Multi-user access			✓

IF YOU INTEND TO BE A SELLER (Premium or Business account) Note that as a seller you need to be able to transfer funds from PayPal to your normal bank account when desired. (PayPal doesn't transfer money into a credit card account.) Make sure that PayPal offers this facility for your particular country. For example, this is not available for South Africa, Sri Lanka and a number of other countries; so a person in one of those countries who wishes to use PayPal for receiving money would need to make some other arrangement to have access to a bank account in a country to which PayPal can transfer money. To see which PayPal transfer facilities are available for your country, go to **www.PayPal.com/worldwide**

Note that only certain 'primary currencies' are listed on the sign-up form, so you may need to select a currency other than your home-country currency.

PayPal's note about South African customers, for example:

Q Can customers in South Africa open a PayPal account?

A As of June 2005, South African residents are able to open a PayPal account, but can only send payments at this time. South African residents may not use PayPal to receive payments. PayPal continues to research how best to expand its offering in South Africa.

8 At the **Account Sign Up** page, fill in all the details required, referring to the prompts and notes as appropriate, including agreeing to the User Agreement and Privacy Policy.

9 When done, click on the **Sign Up** button at the bottom of the page.

Account Sign Up
Personal Account

PayPal Account Owner Contact Information

First Name:

Last Name:

Address Line 1:

Address Line 2: (optional)

Town/City:

County:

Postcode:

Country: United Kingdom

Country of Citizenship: United Kingdom

Home Telephone:

Personal Information
Please enter your name and address as they are listed for your debit card, credit card or bank account.

Mobile Telephone
Enter your mobile phone number to start sending payments and buying items securely from your phone.

A new page will open with instructions on how to confirm your registration when the Welcome e-mail arrives from PayPal. Your PayPal e-mail will most likely include a comment about linking your bank account, and it will read something like this (below left):

Step 2: Get more flexibility – link your bank account

You can link your bank account to your PayPal account and get Verified. Then, you'll be able to:

- Use your bank account to pay for online purchases.
- Transfer money from your PayPal account to your bank account.
- Send unlimited payments.

Your bank account number is safe. You're 100% protected against unauthorized payments sent from your PayPal account.

It's easy to link your bank account – simply log in to your PayPal account and click **Add Bank**.

Note that this option is particularly useful if you intend to sell things online – at eBay auctions, for example – where a balance of funds is likely to build up in your PayPal account. At some stage you will probably want to transfer some of the money to your bank account. Remember, though, that this option is not available in every country (remember the examples of South Africa and Sri Lanka), so check whether your country is able to receive funds in this way. If not, you'll need to find another solution. The Web page to check this is:
www.PayPal.com/worldwide

Once you've activated your account via the e-mail link, you'll be returned to the PayPal website to complete the registration. This last link in the process will take you to your new PayPal account overview page which includes the opportunity to have your account 'verified'. This means adding your credit card details to the PayPal system.

Getting your account verified

On your Account Overview page you'll see a *Status* link with the word *Unverified*. We recommend that you click on that link and follow the verification procedure as this is PayPal's way of giving you more credibility with buyers and sellers alike. There are other benefits too, including a lifting of your funds-sending limit. To find out more about being verified, visit the PayPal help centre and enter the word *verified* into the search facility.

Once you've registered with PayPal, and you have a credit card or debit card, or an acceptable bank account (with available funds) registered with PayPal, you're ready to start buying and paying online with PayPal. And if you've registered for a premier or business account, you're also set up to start selling and receiving money online via PayPal.

FINDING SOLUTIONS TO PAYMENT PROBLEMS

If any problems or transaction disputes should arise, type the word *problem* into the search window at the top of any PayPal Web page to access a page with links to various situations and their suggested solutions.

BEWARE OF SCAM 'PHISHING' E-MAILS There's a fraudulent practice you need to be aware of; it's called *phishing*, pronounced 'fishing'. It involves fraudulently 'fishing' (asking) for confidential information, and it works as follows.

You receive an e-mail or instant message that appears to have been sent by a respected company like PayPal (see PayPal example below), eBay or perhaps even your local bank. The e-mail or message claims that you need to 'validate' your account and it often includes some justification that scares the innocent recipient into responding immediately in order to protect their own online security. They urge you to go to their Web page and log in to your so-called 'account' with your (confidential) username and password. This is just a scam to get your private details so that the fraudsters can access your account and drain your funds.

The e-mail or message usually includes a hyperlink for you to click on to access the 'validation' Web page. **Do not click on it**! Clicking on the link will often result in your computer being infected by a virus.

Never, ever respond to such an email. It is important that you report any phishing attempt to the company whose identity was being used for the scam, e.g. your bank, eBay, PayPal. The PayPal Web page for making such reports is at **https://www.paypal.com/ewf/f=pps_spf**. Alternatively, forward the 'suspect' e-mail to **spoof@paypal.com**. Then delete the e-mail and know that you have just avoided being scammed.

Example of a phishing e-mail:

In the real-life example below we have highlighted in bold some words that are misspelled. Often, fraudulent emails will have spelling and grammar mistakes, though not always. Many of these fraudsters are actually very good at designing Web pages with all the logos and 'look' of the official site they are imitating. So, be warned.

Dear PayPal® customer,

We recently reviewed your account, and we suspect an unauthorized transaction on your account. Protecting your account is our primary concern. As a preventive measure we have **temporary** limited your access to sensitive information.

Paypal features. To ensure that your account is not compromised, simply hit "Resolution Center" to confirm your identity as (a) member of **Paypal**.

    * Login to your **Paypal** with your **Paypal** username and password.

    * Confirm your identity as a card **memeber** of **Paypal**.

Please confirm account information by clicking here Resolution Center and complete the "Steps to Remove Limitations."

*Please do not reply to this message. Mail sent to this address cannot be answered.

Copyright © 1999-2008 PayPal. All rights reserved.

Q How can I tell the difference between a real PayPal email and a fraudulent one?

A The terms spoofing and phishing describe the act of collecting personal information using a fake email with the intention of committing identity theft and Internet fraud. If you click a link included in an email that you're not sure is from PayPal, make certain the address at the top of the browser window that appears reads exactly **www.paypal.com/us**. PayPal email always addresses you by your first and last names, or business name, and **NOT** by Dear PayPal User or Dear PayPal Member.

If you are ever uncertain about the authenticity of the email or the email links, open a new browser window and type in www.paypal.com/us.

If you think you've received a fraudulent email, forward it to spoof@paypal.com and then delete it from your email account.

For the latest tools and information to help protect your identity and avoid fraudulent emails, log in to your PayPal account and click the **Security Center** link at the bottom of any PayPal webpage.

Clicking on the website's Help link and doing a search on the word 'phishing' can usually obtain additional useful information.

LEARN MORE ABOUT PAYPAL

Once you've registered with PayPal (registration is free, remember) we suggest that you take some time clicking on PayPal's various links to learn more about the various features of this service. To get more views from independent sources, you could go to **www.about.com** and to **www.wikipedia.com** and search there for PayPal. You could also use a search engine to search for *opinions about PayPal*, and similar phrases, so that you can get a good feel of what others say about the system.

OTHER PAYMENT OPTIONS

As some people simply cannot obtain a credit card in their own name, there are a few other payment options we should mention. Although our own recommendation would be to pay via PayPal or to make a payment directly to a trusted vendor using a credit card, some people may find these following options to be viable alternatives.

Method	Considerations
Cheque	• The seller must be prepared to accept your cheque. • The cheque must be in a currency that can be deposited in the seller's own country. This method is not as fast as electronic payments because it relies on the postal system and usually requires bank clearance once the cheque has been deposited – which can take a further 10 to 14 days after receipt of the cheque before your purchase can even be shipped to you.
Telegraphic transfer	• This usually involves bank fees for the wire transfer, but it is reasonably fast – if the seller offers this option.
Prepaid debit card (real or virtual)	• These can be purchased online at various service providers' websites. • You must 'load' the card with funds to make it usable, so it requires paying into the account via a credit card or wire transfer, for example. • It's usually quite an expensive option, with the card suppliers charging a premium that is typically anything between 30% and 60% on top of the amount you actually load. • Some cards cannot be topped up. This means that when the available balance runs low, and you cannot deposit funds to top it up, you must buy a new card. So, at that point you may need to pay in two amounts, one from the old card and one from the new card – which is a bit of a pain!

Finding prepaid card suppliers

Prepaid debit cards would not be our strongest recommendation (due to their cost), but in some situations they can definitely serve a useful purpose, particularly for someone who doesn't have or cannot obtain a bank account or a credit card. To find such cards or money transferring services, use your favourite search engine to search for keyword phrases such as *prepaid debit cards*, *prepaid credit cards, money transfer service, send money online*, or similar terms, and browse through the search results that come up. Compare prices as well as terms and conditions, and use your intuition and common sense before ordering.

TIP: CHECK THE OFFERING'S DETAILS CAREFULLY

When choosing a prepaid card, be sure to read the terms and conditions – as well as the fee structure – very carefully so that you know exactly what you're getting and can avoid any nasty surprises later. Note also that some cards are available only in the USA; so check whether the card you're interested in will meet your requirements if you don't live in the USA.

Talk to a banker, an accountant or to Internet-experienced friends

It is often useful to discuss available options with others who may be in the know: like friends who have had some experience with online trading in your country; or a local bank, an accountant, and so on. At the end of the day you are the one who is going to have to make the final decision on what payment method/s will work best for you. Use this chapter's guidelines to help you make that decision.

ALWAYS LOG OUT WHEN YOU'RE DONE Websites that require you to log in (or sign in) do so for your own privacy and/or security protection. Be sure that you always log out before you leave these sites. There's usually a *Log Out* or *Sign Out* link somewhere near the top of the Web page.

ONWARD TO BUYING ONLINE

We've now covered various options for making payments online; and we've shown how to handle a typical registration process for an Internet service involving payment transactions. We've also explained some of the issues to be aware of. What we've covered in this first chapter will stand you in good stead for all chapters that follow. You're now ready to start doing some online buying and selling.

In the next chapter we'll explain how to make a straightforward purchase online. For that, we'll use a safe, trusted and respected website – Amazon.com.

2 Making an online purchase

AMAZON.COM, INC.

For this chapter we'll use a website of one of the early pioneers in the online selling of goods, Amazon.com, Inc. Started in 1994 as an online bookstore, Amazon soon broadened its offering to include other products like video tapes, CDs, computer software, clothing, food, toys and more. If company history and such details are of interest to you, a search for Amazon.com at **www.wikipedia.com** will bring up a lot of information on the company.

Amazon.com headquarters in the PacMed building, Seattle, Washington

SIGN UP AS A CUSTOMER

NOTE: WE'LL USE THE UK WEBSITE SITE FOR THIS TUTORIAL

No matter which of the Amazon websites you register at, your details will be in Amazon's vastly impressive worldwide computer system. This means that you can then log in and shop online at any of their worldwide websites. For the sake of these tutorials we'll register at the Amazon site in the United Kingdom. If you live in a different country that has its own Amazon website, you could follow these steps at your home country's site (see below), adapting as necessary for local page layouts. If your country doesn't have an Amazon website, you could register at a site that's nearest to your country in order to contain the costs of postage when you buy something online.

Amazon websites:

Austria	**www.amazon.at**	Germany	**www.amazon.de**
Canada	**www.amazon.ca**	United Kingdom	**www.amazon.co.uk**
France	**www.amazon.fr**	USA	**www.amazon.com**

1 Go to **www.amazon.co.uk** (or your local Amazon site).
2 Click on the link **New customer? Start here** near the top of the page, to open the **Sign In** page.

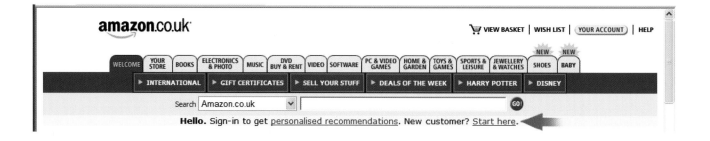

3 On the Sign In page that opens, type a valid email address you'd like to use for your Amazon registration.

4 Click on the radio button next to **No, I am a new custome**r; then click on the button **Sign in using our secure server** to go to the very simple registration page.

5 Enter your **name** (best to give first *and* your last name), as well as a valid **email address**.

6 Enter a **password** that you want to use for this account, and **write it down in a safe place** where you keep all your private login details for various services. (See back of this book.)

7 Click on the **Continue** button.

8 On the **Recommendation Wizard** page that opens, click on one or more of the check-boxes next to the items that interest you the most (e.g. books, DVD, whatever).

9 Click on the **Continue** button.

10 On the next page, fill in the information that will help Amazon give you the best recommendations.

11 Click on the **Continue** button.

12 On next page that opens, click on **Finish**.

Your personalized Amazon *Welcome* page will open, ready for you to start browsing the store and buying.

TIP: OPEN YOUR OWN PAGE

Remember; every time you return to visit an Amazon site, click on the **personalised recommendations** link on the opening page; then, on the page that opens, enter your email address and your password and click on the **Sign in using our secure server** button to launch your own Amazon page (second screenshot that follows).

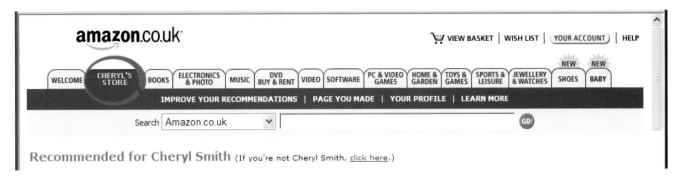

FINDING WHAT YOU'RE LOOKING FOR

The two approaches to buying online at a site like Amazon.com are either to browse around until you see something you want, or to search for the specific item you've heard about because you already know you want to buy it if the price is right.

Browsing around the site

1 To open a drop-down menu of the store's main departments, click on the ▼ **down** arrow next to **Search Amazon.co.uk** (screenshot below left).
2 Click on a department to browse, (we selected *electronics*) then click the ⊙ button.
3 Click on the ▼ **down** arrow next to **Sort by** to arrange the thousands of electronics offered by one of the view options: *bestselling, price* or *customer reviews* (screenshot below right).

Finding a specific item you want

Let's say you want to find a book you've seen with the title *The Really, Really, Really Easy Step-by-step Guide to Digital Photography* (whew!), but you're not sure exactly what the long title is. You remember that it has the words *digital photography* in it, and you think it also has *easy* or *really easy* once or twice in the title. Here's how you might search for the book:

1 Click on the Search window's ⌄ **down** arrow (or the tab at the top of the page) for the department you want to search in (in this example, it's **Books**). (The Search window will now show *Books* instead of *Amazon.co.uk*

2 Press the Tab key to move to the main search text window to the right (or click in it) and type the words **really easy digital photography**

3 Click on GO! or press the Enter key to start the search; the book you're searching for should be displayed on the search results page/s; if not, try again with different search words, or click on **Advanced Search** and fine-tune your search criteria.

With some books on the Amazon sites, there's an opportunity to view some of the inside pages. This option is usually indicated by an icon at the top of the cover image, something like the one on the right.

NOTE: DIFFERENT OFFERINGS AT DIFFERENT AMAZON SITES

Not all of the Amazon sites carry the same items. For example, a particular book you want may not be available from your own country's site, so you would need to order it at a different Amazon site, perhaps the US site, or the site of the publisher's country. What's good is that you can still do this using the same username and password, by simply logging in at the other site.

MAKING THE PURCHASE

1 Click on the book's **title**, or its cover image, to go to a page that displays only that book.

2 Explore any links that interest you, such as **Search inside this book** if that option is available.

3 Look for the **Add to Shopping Basket** button and click on it.

This will take you to another page, often showing other books that have been bought by customers who have purchased the one you've just added to your shopping basket. This allows you to add any of these to your shopping basket too, by simply clicking on the *Add to Basket* button beneath the item you wish to add.

Customers who bought Really, Really, Really Easy Step-by-step Digital Photography (Really Really Really Easy) also bought:

The Really Really Really Easy Step- By-Step Computer Book 1 (XP)
by Gavin Hoole
Price: £6.99 £5.24
Used & new from £2.75
Add to Basket

The Really, Really, Really Easy Step-by-Step Computer Book 2
by Gavin Hoole
Price: £6.99 £5.49
Used & new from £2.45
Add to Basket

The Really, Really, Really Easy Step-by-step Computer Book 2 (XP)
by Gavin Hoole
Price: £6.99 £5.24
Used & new from £3.19
Add to Basket

Your Shopping Basket will update automatically after each addition, showing all the items you've added to your shopping basket thus far, as well as the total value excluding shipping charges.

TIP: AMAZON REMEMBERS WHAT'S IN YOUR BASKET

While you're on your online shopping spree, you can click on as many links and browse as many pages as you wish and Amazon won't lose track of what you've already selected. The system keeps your data in the background all the time. So, you can add new items as you browse around, or – if you have a change of mind – you can even delete items from your basket by clicking the **Edit Shopping Basket** button found under your Subtotal. Once you've finalized your selection and are ready to pay, proceed to the checkout and everything you've added to your basket will be listed.

The selected items that you've not yet paid for remain in your Shopping Cart for 90 days – even after you've logged out and left the site. So it's not essential that you make your purchase immediately after selecting an item. You can return any time within the 90 days to finalize the purchase, or to delete an item and buy something else if you've since changed your mind.

TIP: THE AMAZON 'WISH LIST' OPTION

A *Wish List* is a personalized list of the things you'd love to have from an Amazon website – much like a *Wedding Gift Registry* that a future bride and groom would set up at a store so that friends can select from a list of their desired wedding gifts. When you find something at an Amazon website that you'd like to receive, click on the **Add to my Wish List** button under the blue boxes on the right-hand side of each product information page. You'll then be prompted to add further information to your Wish List.

You can also find out what friends have on their Wish Lists and buy an item for them as a gift. On the Wish List page, type in the name or e-mail address of the person you're looking for. When their Wish List is displayed, select the item you'd like to buy for them, as well as your gift-wrapping and delivery preferences; then click on the **Add to Basket** button. Amazon will send your gift to the recipient on your behalf, wrapped as per your request.

Checking out and paying

1 When you've completed your shopping selections, click on the **Proceed to Checkout** button to go to the **Checkout Sign In** page where you may need to enter your email address and your password again, as a security measure.

2 Fill in the address you'd like your order to be delivered to (it doesn't have to be your own address, but could be that of a friend if you're sending the item as a gift), and phone number; then click on the **Continue** button to go to the **Delivery Options** page.

3 Select your delivery option; then click the **Continue** button to go the first **Checkout: Payment** page.

4 If you're paying by credit card, click on the **down** arrow to select your type of card, and accurately type the card details – as shown on the card – into the various text fields (already explained in Chapter 1).

Pay with new card   Credit Card No.   Cardholder's Name   Expiry Date

Amazon.co.uk MasterCard
Amazon.co.uk MasterCard
Visa/Delta/Electron
MasterCard/EuroCard
American Express
Switch/Solo/Maestro
(or cheque funds on account)

Number: OR Start Date: --- / ---

rder

5   Click on the **Continue** button to open the second **Checkout: Payment** page where you need to enter your invoice address.

6   Read the details as you've entered them on this last page and go back to make any necessary changes before you place your order.

7   If everything looks correct, click on the **Place your order** button.

NOTE: AMAZON DOES NOT ACCEPT PAYPAL

If you've set up a PayPal account for yourself, note that you cannot use it at any of the Amazon stores. But don't despair; you'll definitely be able to use it at eBay and many other sites. If you don't have a credit card, you'll need to choose from the payment method options given in the Help section at the Amazon sites. Each country's site has its own payment options which may differ from country to country.

NOTE: PAYING FOR AN ITEM USING A GIFT CERTIFICATE

If you've received an Amazon gift certificate, be aware that you can only use the certificate at the site from which the certificate was purchased, For example, you cannot use an Amazon gift certificate at the US Amazon.com site if the certificate was purchased from Amazon.co.uk.

BUYING ON AN AMAZON MARKETPLACE

On Amazon's *Marketplace*, you can buy new, used and collectable items from third-party sellers (not from Amazon itself), and you can do this from the same page on which you can buy from Amazon.

1   In the **More Buying Choices** box on the right of each product information page, click on the link for **used and new** items.

2   Follow the page prompts to access a new or used item from a third party.

3   When you're ready to buy, place your order and the item will be dispatched directly to you by the third-party seller.

RELAX! PAYMENT TO THIRD PARTIES IS HANDLED BY AMAZON

Don't be concerned about sending your credit/debit card or bank details to the stranger who's selling the item, because payment is handled via *Amazon Payments*, which is a safe and secure payment system offered and managed by Amazon themselves.

Once you've completed all the purchasing steps you can sit back and wait for your purchase to arrive at the address you specified. Easy as pie!

NEXT: BUYING AT ONLINE AUCTIONS

Now that you have a good feel of how straightforward online buying is done, the next thing we'll tackle will be how to bid and buy at an online auction.

3 Buying at online auctions

Buying goods at online stores like Amazon.com is a very convenient way of shopping from the comfort of your own home. But once you add auction bidding to the process, a whole new emotional dynamic starts to take place – in fact many people find it so much fun to bid at an online auction that they can't wait to bid again at another auction.

When someone mentions online auctions it's not surprising that the name eBay immediately comes to mind. Launched as AuctionWeb in 1995 by computer programmer Pierre Omidyar, eBay Inc. rapidly grew to become the largest online trading site in the world. Every day of the week, eBay's over 200 million users can choose from more than 100 million listed items on their websites. eBay's auctions listings cover virtually anything that can be auctioned legally, from cell phones, CDs, dolls and clothing, to computers, power boats and motor vehicles. If someone wants it, you can be sure there will be someone ready to sell it on eBay.

eBay owns several other well-known companies too, including the respected service companies of PayPal and Skype. In short, eBay is huge and extremely popular. So it's only natural that this should be the site we've chosen for our tutorials about online auctions. If you know how to bid, buy and sell on eBay, then you'll be able to find your way around any other online auction site too.

HOW TO BUY ON eBAY – A BROAD OVERVIEW

1 First, decide what it is you wish to buy.

2 Register as an eBay member (free).

3 Search the website for the item – several similar items may be listed.

4 Select the specific item that interests you.

5 Read all the details – description, shipping and any other charges, returns policy, etc.

6 Check out the seller's credentials and read the comments made by others who have already bought things from this seller.

7 Start bidding (or pay the *Buy It Now* fixed price if this option is offered and you really want the item and are therefore prepared to pay the *Buy It Now* price).

8 If your bid/immediate purchase is successful, pay for the item and take delivery of it when it arrives.

That's it, in a nutshell. The rest of this chapter goes into more detail on how to follow this process, together with useful tips, hints and explanations along the way.

REGISTER ON eBAY

You can browse as a visitor on any of the eBay websites to view all the offerings and click on the information links. But once you want to start trading on eBay you do need to register as an eBay user. Registration is free to anyone aged 18 years or older. Let's register now.

---

1   Go to **www.ebay.com** and click on the Register button.

NOTE: IF YOU USE A FREE WEB-BASED E-MAIL ADDRESS

You will need a valid e-mail address to register at eBay. If you use a free Web-based email address (e.g. Yahoo!, Hotmail or Gmail), you must place a valid credit card number on file at eBay to verify your identity. Your card will be used for identification only and will not be charged.

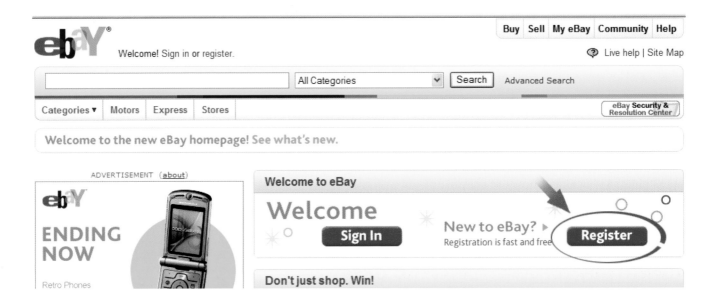

2   On the page that opens, fill in your personal details as with any typical online registration form.

3   Click on the **Country or region ⌄ down** arrow to select your country. (If it's not shown in that initial short list, click on **See all countries...** and on the next page select your country and click on the **Change country or region** button.)

4   Decide on a **User ID and password** you will use for eBay, then write them down and put them somewhere safe so that you have an off-computer record in case you need to refer to them later.

5 Enter your **User ID and password**.

6 Pick a secret question and answer so that eBay can verify your identity should you forget your password in the future.

7 Click on **User Agreement** and read through the whole agreement so that you're familiar with eBay's rules and modus operandi; also click on **Privacy Policy** and read that carefully too.

8 To accept eBay's terms and conditions, click in the check-box next to **I agree that:**.

9 When you've completed all the required fields, click on **Register** to receive a confirmation e-mail from eBay.

10 In the e-mail you'll receive from eBay (see example below), click on the **Activate Now** button to confirm your registration.

 eBay sent this message to Jesse Smith (jessesmith2001).
Your registered name is included to show this message originated from eBay. Learn more.

Complete your eBay registration

Hi jessesmith2001,

Just click "Activate Now" to complete your registration. That's all there is to it. After that, you are ready to start shopping!

This is the last step, we promise!

Activate Now

If the above link does not work:
1. Write down this confirmation code: pLSoW
2. Type in or copy and paste this link into your Web browser:
http://cgi4.ebay.ca/ws/eBayISAPI.dll?RegisterConfirmCode&onepagereg=1&runame=
3. Enter your confirmation code.

If you need additional help, contact eBay's Customer Support or Live Help

E-mail received from eBay as a final step for activating your account

You will then be returned to the eBay Welcome page. Once your registration has been confirmed and activated, you're ready to start bidding and buying on eBay.

NOTE: YOUR REGISTRATION WORKS ON ALL eBAY SITES

No matter which country you selected during the registration process, your eBay user ID will work on every eBay site worldwide. You can therefore bid and buy on any site outside your own country of residence – provided that the seller has checked the **Ship Worldwide** box to indicate a willingness to ship to other destination countries. Many people, in fact, do just that.

SIGN IN BEFORE YOU DO ANYTHING ELSE

Before you even start browsing the eBay site for bargains, always sign in first with your User ID and password so that you can access your *My eBay* page to check for updates of:

- new messages
- new eBay announcements
- current *specials* (related to areas your past bidding indicates you might be interested in)
- the status of any bids that you have pending, and so on.

1 If your *My eBay* isn't the page that opens, click on the **My eBay** tab at the top right of the Web page. (See below for an example of a *My eBay* page.)

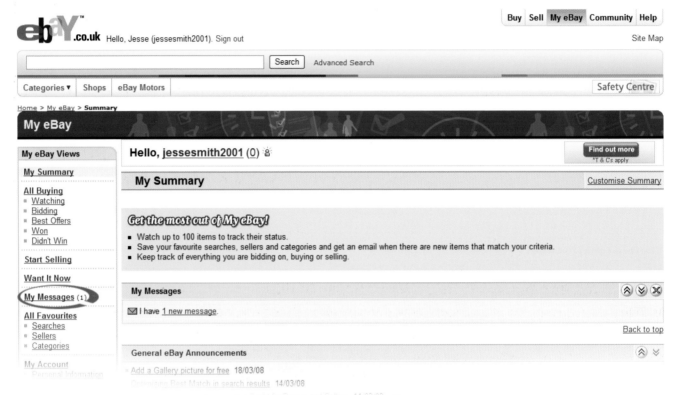

A typical new member's *My eBay* page

NOTE: HOW EBAY MARKS THE MESSAGES

Messages from eBay are highlighted with a pale green background. Messages from other members, such as questions about an item, are not highlighted. Unread messages are shown in bold. You can delete messages whenever you want to.

2 To access your messages, click on the **My Messages** link on your *My eBay* page (see screen shot below).

BROWSING AROUND TO SEE WHAT'S ON OFFER

As with Amazon.com and other online store sites, on eBay you can click on a category and browse through its sub-categories to see if there are any items that interest you. If you find an item you might want to bid on, click on it for more details.

There are various ways to browse categories of items. Here are some step-by-step suggestions.

To show all the categories with their active sub-categories:

1 Click on the Categories▼ tab to display a list of all the main categories, each with its own active sub-categories shown beneath it; this view requires that you scroll down the page to see all the main categories and some of their active sub-categories.

To expand a category further to display *all* of its sub-categories:

2 Click on a category's **bold heading** to display *all* the sub-categories within that category.

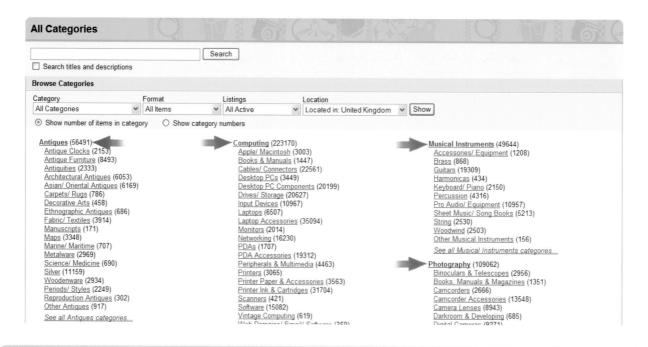

NOTE: THE NUMBERS SHOWN IN BRACKETS

The numbers shown in brackets behind the category and sub-category headings indicate the number of items currently up for auction or for sale in that category or sub-category.

With over 100,000,000 items available on eBay on any given day, browsing around in this way can take a lot of time if you don't drill down to sub-categories of sub-categories until you get to the smallest relevant group you wish to explore for items to buy. Doing searches for a specific item (next topic) is often a much quicker way of finding exactly what you want – provided of course that you already know exactly what you want.

SEARCHING FOR A SPECIFIC ITEM

If you know exactly what item you're looking for, you can bypass the categories sequence by doing an item-specific search like this:

1 At the top of any eBay page, type a description of the item you're looking for – e.g. **Ovation acoustic guitar** – into the Search window and click on **Search** (or press the Enter ↵ key) and wait for the search results to load.

Narrowing your search down even further

Every eBay customer will find their own preferred way of quickly searching for what they want to buy, but here's a useful method you can use to narrow down your search even further. Let's assume you're looking for an item (e.g. a guitar) that must meet the following criteria:

- It must be an *acoustic* guitar;
- You want to pay for it using your PayPal account (eBay's preferred method);

- You want to buy it from a UK seller;
- You're more interested in bidding on an item that is ending within the next 24 hours.

You would then use the *Search Options* section of the left-hand pane of the results to narrow your search down to include these additional criteria too (see screenshot below right).

NOTE: AUCTION DURATION

An auction can run for 1, 3, 5, 7 or 10 days, as decided by the seller.

---

1 Click in the applicable **check-boxes** to make your selections.

2 Click on the **Show Items** button at the bottom to display the search results.

3 In the search results, for more details of the item that interests you, **click** on its **title**.

Example of results from a narrowed search:

When you narrow down your search in this way fewer items will be displayed, and they will all be more relevant to your specific needs (see screenshot below).

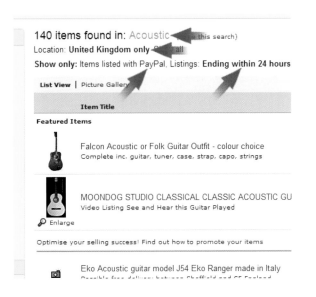

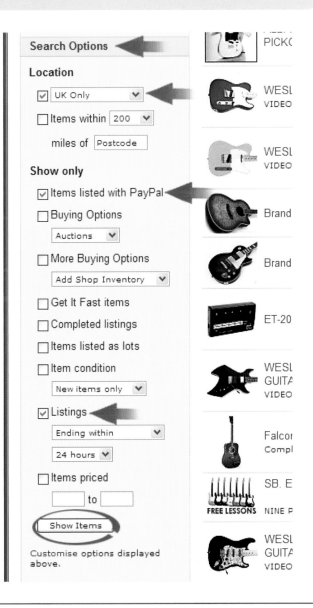

CHOOSE THE APPROPRIATE COUNTRY Be sure to select a country for your search that is appropriate to your needs and to the item you intend bidding on. If the value is not too high, and the item can be mailed at a relatively low cost, then buying from another country may be fine. But if it is a bulky or heavy item, or highly-priced, you may want to consider the various issues involved, including any risks that might be associated with an international purchase.

TIP: PHOTOS MAKE AN OFFER MORE ATTRACTIVE

Notice how having photographs of an item makes it so much easier to get a good idea of what the item looks like: its colour, condition, and so on. Remember this when you become a seller yourself (next chapter).

TIP: FIND WHICH SEARCH METHOD WORKS BEST FOR YOU

There are many routes to finding the item you're looking for; we've shown only some of these. The method you use for your own searches will naturally depend on how certain you are about the specifics of the item you're looking for, and several other factors too. So don't feel that there is only one 'correct' search method. Use whatever suits your own needs at the time. In addition, we suggest that you explore all the search options available and see where they take you.

CHECK OUT THE SELLER'S CREDENTIALS

There's no point in getting excited about bidding on the item before you've decided whether or not the seller seems like someone you're comfortable doing business with. So we recommend that before entering a bid, you review the seller's credentials.

1 Once you've clicked on the item that interests you, in the **Meet the seller** section on the right of the Web page, note the **Feedback** stats – e.g. 100% Positive, as shown in the next screenshot.

2 Click on the **See detailed feedback** link just below that, then click the **Feedback as a buyer** tab to read other buyers' comments about this seller. This will tell you what kind of comments and opinions resulted in the overall feedback rating.

3 Click on the other links in that section to read more details.

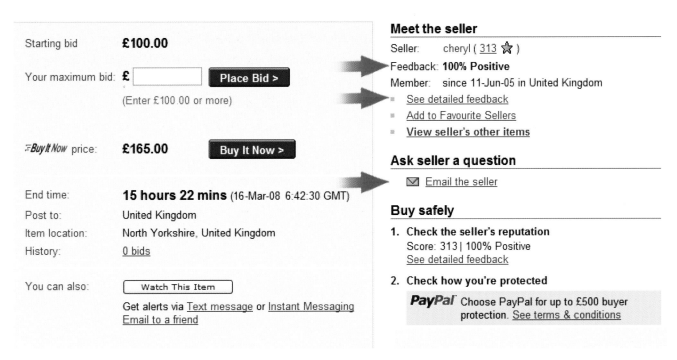

Above left: Details of the selected item

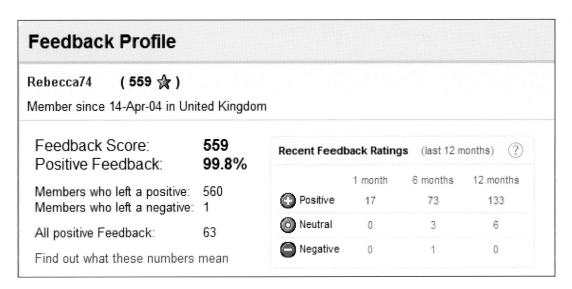

Above: A typical Feedback Profile layout

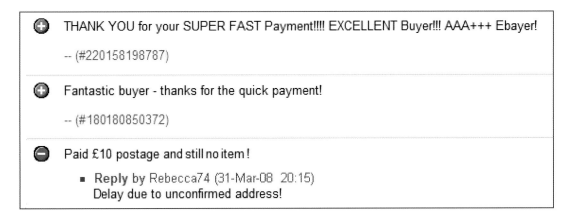

Example of Buyer feedback comments with the Seller's response to a negative comment

CHECK THE ITEM DESCRIPTION AND SELLING TERMS

1 Scroll down the item's Web page to view a more detailed description of the item on offer.

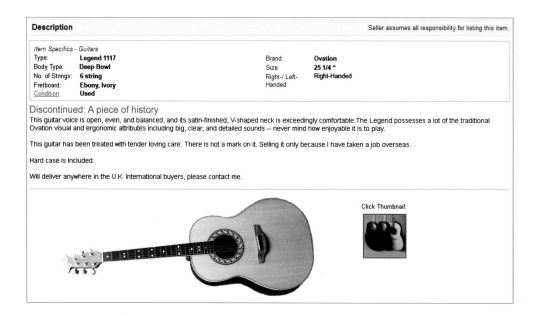

2 Click on any extra links and photo thumbnails for more details and images.

3 If this is the item you definitely want to own, scroll down further to read the other details on the Web page.

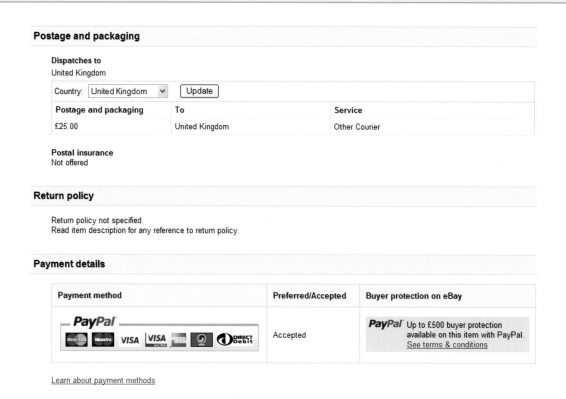

TIP: YOU CAN E-MAIL THE SELLER IF NECESSARY

If there's something important that you wish to clarify before you decide to bid and it's not mentioned anywhere in the item's details, you can click on the **Email the seller** link in the **Meet the seller section** (see screenshot top of page 37) to ask the seller for the missing information. A prompt and informative response from the seller can be an indication of good customer service.

WHAT THE NOTES IN THE 'BIDS' COLUMN MEAN

You may have noticed on the items list a column headed *Bids*, with some characters or icons opposite each item in the listing (see screenshot below). The table below this screenshot explains what each of these notes means.

Item Title	Bids	Price*	Postage to GBR		Time Left
Featured Items					
Fender Jaguar Custom	- *Buy It Now*	£425.00 £550.00	£25.00	P	2h 57m
BLACK LEATHER GUITAR STRAP	-	£6.97		P	1h 27m
KACES XPRESS SERIES BASS GUITAR GIG BAG *NEW*	*Buy It Now*	£19.95	Free	P	5d 09h 56m
3 PICKUP PEARL SCRATCH PLATE	*Buy It Now or Best Offer*	£35.00	£5.50	P	2d 20h 35m
1950s Archtop f hole guitar	4	£62.00	£15.00	P	10h 02m

Notes in the *Bids* column	What they mean
A **hyphen** (-) together with the *Buy It Now* icon	A hyphen indicates that no bids have yet been placed. Start bidding, or buy and pay immediately at the *Buy It Now* price shown
A **hyphen** (-) only	You can only bid; no *Buy It Now* option; and no bids have been offered yet
Buy It Now icon only	No bidding; only buy and pay now
Buy It Now or Best Offer icon	Buy at the price stated, or make an offer I can't refuse
A ***Number*** only	The number of bids placed thus far; no *Buy It Now* option

The next few topics give a more detailed explanation of these bid-or-buy options that appear on eBay pages next to the items up for auction.

UNDERSTANDING THE SELLER'S SELLING OPTIONS

As noted above, there are various options available to sellers on eBay and you'll need to understand these so that you can make the best bidding or buying decisions.

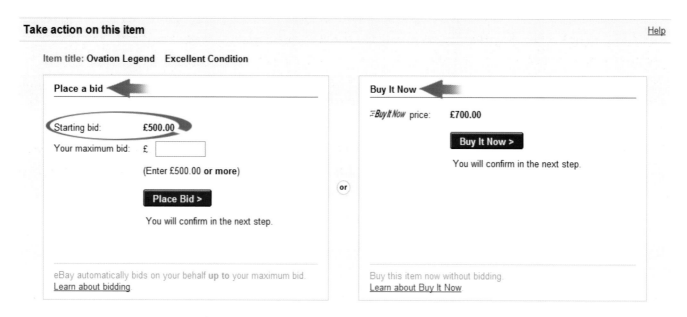

Auction-style listings

An auction-style listing is similar to an offline auction that one can attend in person at an auction house. Here are some of the aspects of an online auction-style listing.

Starting bid (left-hand column in the screenshot above): This is the price at which bidding for an auction-style item must begin. (If people have already started bidding, the heading will change to *Current bid*.) For your bid to be accepted it must be at least equal to the *Starting bid* or higher than the Current bid amount.

Your maximum bid: You need to decide the maximum price you are prepared to pay for the item. If you are really keen on winning the auction and owning the item, your *Maximum bid* may well be quite a bit above the *Starting* or *Current bid* level. If someone bids higher than your maximum bid at the time the auction closes, they will win the auction and get the item. During the course of the auction, you can increase your maximum bid to outbid a new highest bid from someone else, but you may never reduce it.

Reserve price: Sometimes a seller will choose to set a secret minimum price that s/he is prepared to accept for the item (usually used for higher-value items). The reserve price is never visible to buyers; only the seller and eBay know what it is. Any bid that is below the reserve will not be accepted and the bidder must submit a higher bid until the reserve is met. Once the reserve has been met, the term *Current bid* will appear as the new minimum amount that may be bid.

≡Buy It Now   **The Buy It Now option**

The *Buy It Now* icon represents an option that some sellers offer. The *Buy It Now* price is the price the seller will accept for immediate sale, and it is only available if no valid bids have already been made. Any buyer who wants to secure the item without going through the bidding process can offer the *Buy It Now* price displayed and must pay for the item immediately. This effectively ends the auction there and then.

NOTE: ANY ACCEPTABLE BID CANCELS THE *BUY IT NOW* OPTION

As soon as someone places a bid that equals or exceeds any reserve price (or **starting bid** price) that the buyer may have set, the *Buy It Now* option falls away, the icon disappears and the item must now be sold by auction. Therefore, while you are still considering whether to buy it now or place a bid (in the hope of getting the item a bit cheaper), it is quite possible that someone else may either place an acceptable bid or complete their own *Buy It Now* transaction ahead of you and knock you out of the race. So, if you do intend to buy the item at the Buy It Now price, make sure you move quickly to complete your transaction.

YOUR BID OR *BUY IT NOW* REQUEST IS A BINDING CONTRACT Once you start to bid, you have entered into a binding contract. If yours is the winning bid you're obliged to complete the transaction and pay for the item. The same applies when you confirm that you wish to *Buy It Now;* in this case payment is due immediately.

Classified Ads

There is also a *Classified Ads* option which is an online version of the typical classified adverts one sees in newspapers and some magazines. The seller lists what he has to sell and interested buyers contact the seller directly via the seller's contact details given on the item's Web page. No bidding takes place and the transaction is handled directly with the seller, not through eBay's auctions or *Buy It Now* systems.

TIP: TO LEARN MORE

To find out more about the various buying and selling formats offered by eBay, click on the **Help** tab (top right of any page) and in the Help Pages search window, type the words **buying formats** then click on the **Search Help Pages** button.

TIP: eBAY'S GLOSSARY OF TERMS

Another useful link is the one to the **eBay Glossary**. If you're not sure what an eBay term means, go to this Web page: **http://pages.ebay.co.uk/help/newtoebay/glossary.html**. Many of the explanations there also include extra links to more detailed and related information.

YOU CAN NARROW YOUR SEARCH TO A BUYING FORMAT THAT SUITS YOU

If there is a particular selling format you want to buy with, then:

1 On the page that lists the items you've searched for, click on the applicable **tab** of your choice: **All Items** (displays all categories); or **Auctions** (auction-style listings only); or **Buy It Now** (only items having this option); or **Classified Ads** (displays only items advertised in the Classifieds).

NOTE: A GREYED-OUT TAB INDICATES NO LISTINGS

If a particular kind of selling option has no items listed, of the kind you specified in your search, this will be indicated by a greyed-out tab (e.g. the Classified Ads tab in the screenshot above).

In the topics that follow, we'll explain how to use the two main auction options: bidding and buying it now. We'll start with the bidding option.

eBAY'S PROXY BIDDING SYSTEM

eBay has a very useful automatic system of updating bids on your behalf as soon as someone outbids you. It's called the *proxy bidding* system and is quite safe – that is, you will never pay more than what you've entered as your *maximum bid*.

HOW THE *PROXY BIDDING* PROCESS WORKS

For single-item auctions, eBay operates an automated *proxy bidding* system. This means that once you've entered your maximum bid eBay takes over the bidding on your behalf. If someone subsequently bids higher than you, eBay increases your bid just enough to beat that new bid. Your own *maximum* amount is not revealed to other bidders or to the seller; and eBay's system never increases your new bid beyond your stated maximum bid. All that the seller and other bidders will see is your new bid, entered automatically for you by eBay as your proxy. eBay will keep bidding on your behalf in this way until your maximum bid is reached.

If another bidder enters a bid (or a maximum bid) that is higher than your own maximum bid, eBay will advise you by e-mail that yours is no longer the highest bid in the system. You can then decide whether you wish to increase your current bid in order to remain in the auction. If your bid is the highest bid at the close of the auction, you win the auction and the item is yours – even if your winning bid is less than the maximum amount you were willing to go to. You could, in fact, end up paying much less than your maximum bid amount, if no one else has a higher maximum bid than yours.

eBay's automatic *proxy* bidding feature saves you the hassle of continuously checking in to re-bid every time someone else has placed a higher bid. The *proxy bidding* system also ensures that each new bid eBay makes on your behalf is just enough to beat the latest competitive bid, and no more. In other words, if you are outbid, eBay doesn't automatically increase your bid right up to your maximum bid level. It re-bids little by little, just enough as is necessary each time for you to become the highest bidder again.

eBay's proxy bid increments range on a scale from a few pence/cents to around £100/$100 according to the level of the price being bid. To see eBay's current table of bid increments, click on the *Help* tab (top right of any eBay Web page), and in the *Help* search window do a search for the words *bid increments*.

Start bidding

1 Type your **maximum bid** amount into the text window and click on the **Place Bid >** button to go to the **Review and Confirm Bid** window. (You still have one more chance to change your mind about whether or not to bid for the item, but once you've confirmed your bid – next step – that's it, you're committed, unless/until your maximum bid is beaten by another bidder.)

Take action on this item

Item title: OVATION CELEBRITY DELUX

Place a bid

Starting bid: £150.00

Your maximum bid:£ [200.00] (Enter £150.00 **or more**)

[Place Bid >]   You will confirm in the next step.

NOTE: TO START BIDDING YOU MUST BE SIGNED IN

You should already have signed in to eBay, but if you haven't done so, you need to do that before you can confirm your bid in the next steps.

---

2 Check all the details of your bid carefully, to make sure you haven't made a typing error.

3 When you're ready to activate your bid, click on the **Confirm Bid** button.

Review and Confirm Bid

Hello jessesmith2001 (Not you?)

Item you're bidding on:
OVATION GUITAR
Current bid: £150.00
Your maximum bid: **£200.00**
Shipping and handling: Check item description and payment instructions or contact seller for details.
Payment methods: PayPal, Cheque.

By clicking on the button below, you commit to buy this item from the seller if you're the winning bidder.

You are agreeing to a contract -- You will enter into a legally binding contract to purchase the item from the seller if you're the winning bidder. You are responsible for reading the full item listing, including the seller's instructions and accepted payment methods. Seller assumes all responsibility for listing this item.

eBay will enter your bid into the system automatically, confirm your bid, monitor the bidding process for you and operate its proxy bidding on your behalf.

Immediately outbid?

If someone has entered a *maximum bid* that is higher than your own starting maximum bid, eBay's *Bid Confirmation* window will indicate that immediately and give you the opportunity to bid again – that is, to raise your own *maximum bid*. Once you've entered a successful maximum bid, eBay will enter a bid on your behalf that is marginally above the current highest bid, to place you in the lead as the person with the latest highest bid.

If someone later bids higher than the bid entered by eBay on your behalf, eBay will increase your bid just enough to place it marginally above that other bidder's bid, but eBay will never increase your bid above the price you entered as *Your maximum bid*.

eBay's automatic proxy bidding process continues until the closing time of that auction, or until your maximum bid is reached, at which time you'll be asked if you wish to increase your maximum bid in order to stay in the auction and try to secure the item.

TIP: YOU CAN KEEP TRACK OF YOUR BIDS

To keep track of what's happening with your bids, you can click on the **My eBay** tab to go to the <u>All Buying</u> section on the left of the *My eBay* window.

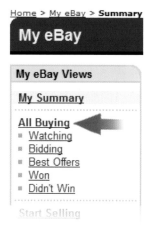

TIP: SAVE THE WEB PAGE FOR FUTURE REFERENCE

It's always a good idea to keep a copy of the Web page showing all the details of the item you bid on. This can come in handy later when you wish to check that the item you received is exactly as described on the eBay Web page. It's particularly useful if you become a frequent bidder/buyer and wish to keep the details of several items you've bid on, so that you're well equipped in the event of any subsequent dispute.

---

1 In your Web browser (e.g. Internet Explorer) click on **File** then **Save As...**
2 In the **Save Webpage** dialog box that opens, browse to a suitable folder (or create a new folder) to which you want to save the Web page.
3 Accept the name given by eBay and click on **Save**.

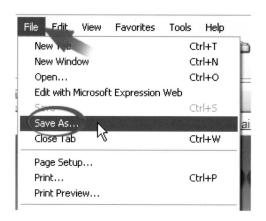

AT THE END OF THE AUCTION

At the close of the auction, eBay will send you an e-mail to tell you whether or not you've won the bidding. If you have, the e-mail will include details of the next steps you need to take. In summary, these are:

1 Receive eBay confirmation: eBay sends an email to notify you that you have won the item and to pay now (only pay if you know the shipping and handling costs which are not always shown for International buyers).

2 Receive seller's confirmation: The seller should send you an email notifying you of the total cost including shipping and handling costs. (If you are an International buyer, the shipping costs may not have been quoted on the auction page.)

3 Make payment: Follow the seller's payment requirements and effect your payment accordingly. Most sellers accept PayPal which allows the buyer to pay online instantly with a credit card or bank account.

4 Receive the item you bought: The seller ships the goods to the address you specified.

Making payment (step 2 above)

If you select PayPal as your payment method, a window will open for you to log in to your PayPal account at the PayPal website (or register with PayPal if you haven't yet done so). Once you've completed the payment transaction, a PayPal payment confirmation will be displayed, and the transaction has now been finalized.

LEAVE FEEDBACK FOR THE SELLER

eBay has a feedback system for both buyers and sellers to receive comments based on the transaction just completed. These feedback comments help both buyers and sellers alike, and are an extremely useful part of an online auction system.

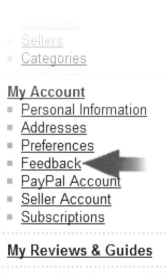

Once you've received the item/s you've bought on the auction, be sure to leave your own feedback for your seller. And remember, feedback works both ways: buyer to seller and vice versa. You can access the Feedback link via the *My Account* link on your *My eBay* page (see screenshot extract on the right).

Leaving your feedback:

1 After logging in, click on the **My eBay** tab.

2 Click on **Feedback** to view recent feedback you've received and also any reminders of feedback you still need to give.

3 Click on **Leave Feedback** to submit your feedback rating and any comments.

If you're dissatisfied:

1 If you're not happy about some aspect of your latest transaction, rather than leave negative feedback it's best that you first contact the seller to try and resolve the problem. Often it is simply a matter of miscommunication or misunderstanding that can be resolved through direct contact.

If you can't reach a solution with the other party:

1 At the bottom of any eBay Web page click on the link **eBay Security and Resolution Center**.

2 Use the tools available at the Centre to try to resolve the problem.

NOTE: eBAY'S EVOLVING FEEDBACK SYSTEM

Auction websites such as eBay are constantly striving to improve their systems and site functions. Feedback is one such area that is always under attention to ensure that it is fair to both buyers and sellers. Members have expressed concerns about unfair negative feedback and also about feedback given in retaliation to what is seen as fair criticism. Be sure to comply with the current eBay rules when it comes to offering feedback on a transaction.

HOW TO BE A SMART BIDDER

1 **Bid later rather than sooner** (known as *Snipe Bidding*): The sooner you start bidding the more likely you are to help drive the final price higher as other bidders respond and bid against you with their first bid and via the subsequent eBay *proxy bidding* system. Experienced bidders therefore wait till near the end of the auction before placing their first bid – even as late as the last few minutes before the auction closes.

2 **Bid at a realistic price – not too low and not too high**: If you know what you're looking for on the auction, do some homework before you start looking for an item you want to bid on. Check your local newspaper classifieds, other websites, and so on to get an idea of the prices that similar items are being sold for. Then, when it's time to bid, be realistic. If it's not so important that you win the bid, then by all means bid on the lower side in the hope that you can get a bargain. If it's important for you to have the item, then bid high enough to stand a good chance of winning the auction – but don't go 'over the top' and bid an unrealistically high price.

3 **Bid with your head, not too much with your emotions**: Keep your maximum price realistic and try to keep a steady mind. Some people are more prone than others to getting swept up in the competitive feeling, and they may lose sight of the price they were originally prepared to pay. As with any offline auction, the impulse to win the auction and beat the competition can sometimes heat up, especially towards the last few minutes of the auction. Sometimes this can result in people paying quite a lot more than they really intended to pay in the first place. So, try to keep your cool and bid sensibly whilst still having fun.

4   Factor in the shipping and handling charges: Before you start bidding, check what additional costs are specified in the item's description. As they say, read the small print. Decide the absolute maximum **cost** you're prepared to incur to get the item into your home if you should win the auction. Then deduct any shipping/packaging/handling charges (which may be shown separately) from that absolute maximum 'budget', and make that lower amount the absolute highest bid you will make on the auction. That way there won't be any surprises and you won't end up paying more than you expected. Scroll down to the bottom of the Item Description to the section on shipping, payment details and return policy, and make sure you take into account the following items:

- Shipping and handling costs
- Method of shipment
- Seller's guarantee and/or return policies
- Methods of payment

THE *BUY IT NOW* OPTION (where offered)

If you've decided that you really want the item, and you're prepared to pay the *Buy It Now* price for it (where the seller offers this option), follow the steps on the next page (after reading the notes in these next two important text boxes).

NOTE: DO YOU QUALIFY AS A *BUY IT NOW* BUYER?

You may only use the *Buy It Now* option if you meet at least one of the following two criteria:
- Have an overall net feedback rating of zero or higher (see **Scoring system** explanation below); or
- Have a valid credit card or debit card registered on eBay's system.

If you do not yet qualify you will be prompted to give effect to one of these criteria, after which you can buy the item and pay the *Buy It Now* price immediately. The listing will then end immediately and you will have purchased the item you want.

Scoring system for comments left for you by others:

+1 point   for each positive comment

0 points   for each neutral comment

-1 point   for each negative comment

A star   once you've received 10 or more comments and ratings

 THE PRICE EXCLUDES POSTAGE AND PACKAGING CHARGES Note that the *Buy It Now* price does not include postage and packaging charges. Because immediate payment is required, for *Buy It Now* listings these P&P costs and any other charges are noted separately in the item's details. If you're unsure, you should contact the seller to find out the total cost of having the item shipped to your location.

How to *Buy it now*

1 Skip the bidding option and click on the **Buy It Now** button.

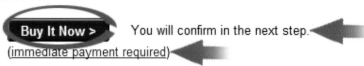

Buy It Now

Buy It Now price:£850.00

Buy It Now >
(immediate payment required)

You will confirm in the next step.

The seller requires you to make immediate payment to claim this item. You will be asked to do so with PayPal on the next page. Learn more.

Buy this item now without bidding. Learn about Buy It Now.

2 Click on **Commit to Buy** and follow the prompts to effect your payment so that the seller can pack the item and ship it to you (by mail, courier, transporter, depending on the arrangement made).

Review and Commit to Buy

Hello jessesmith2001 (Not you?)

Item you're buying:
OVATION GUITAR

Buy It Now price: £850.00

Payment methods: PayPal, Cheque, Demand draft, Other - See Payment Instructions.

By clicking on the button below, you commit to buy this item from the seller.

Commit to Buy

You are agreeing to a contract -- You will enter into a legally binding contract to purchase the item from the seller. You are responsible for reading the full item listing, including the seller's instructions and accepted payment methods. Seller assumes all responsibility for listing this item.

Concluding the transaction

Once you've committed to buying at the *Buy It Now* price, complete the transaction in much the same way as when winning an auction; and remember to leave your feedback comments once you've received the goods you've purchased.

'SPOOF' E-MAILS PURPORTEDLY FROM eBAY If an e-mail affects your eBay account, you'll find a copy in *My Messages*. Therefore, if you receive an e-mail that appears to come from eBay about a problem with your account, or requests for personal information, account updates or verification, and there is not a copy of that e-mail in the *My Messages* section of your *My eBay* page, then it's definitely a fake e-mail and not from eBay.

We strongly recommend that you go through eBay's various explanations about spoof e-mail. You'll learn how to spot a spoof e-mail and also a fake website purporting to be part of eBay. You'll also learn what to do about spoofs and how to protect your eBay account from this kind of fraud. The eBay URL is: http://pages.ebay.com/education/spooftutorial

NEXT: SELLING AT AN eBAY AUCTION

We've now covered buying online. In Chapter 1, we used Amazon as a typical online store site and in this chapter we've explained how to buy at an online eBay auction. In the next chapter we'll look at how you can sell your own items on an eBay auction.

4 Selling at online auctions

You're already familiar with many of the eBay terms used, such as starting price, maximum bid, auction-style and *Buy It Now* listings, and you also have a feel of how to navigate your way around an eBay website. In this chapter we'll extend that knowledge further and work through an auction from the seller's side of a transaction, and give the how-to steps applicable to selling an item on an eBay auction.

Assuming you have already registered as a buyer on eBay, there are a few additional steps that are needed in order to become a registered seller as well; but first, here's an overview of selling on eBay.

HOW TO SELL ON eBAY – A BROAD OVERVIEW

1 Register as a seller (free).

2 Sign up to accept the payment method appropriate for your country.

3 Browse through the list of completed sales of items similar to yours to get ideas for your own listing.

4 Take a suitable digital photo of your item to enhance your chances of a successful auction.

5 Decide the starting price, whether you want to set a reserve, and so on.

6 Work out the postage/shipping and packaging costs for inclusion in your listing.

7 Enter all the details needed to get your item listed, and activate your listing.

8 When the item is sold, complete the transaction with your customer.

9 Keep your customer informed by e-mail to ensure good customer service.

10 On receipt of payment from your customer, dispatch the item promptly and advise your customer of the shipment details.

11 Enter feedback details for your customer and request the same for yourself.

This chapter will take you through each of these processes so that you can quickly become a successful auction seller on eBay. You can then adapt this knowledge to any other online auction site you wish to trade at.

 WEB PAGES DO VARY FROM SITUATION TO SITUATION Remember, eBay (and other online auction sites too) may have different Web page layouts for their different country-specific sites. In addition, Web pages are generally dynamic; content changes daily, and layouts change from time to time too. For these reasons, what you see on your computer screen when you work through these procedures may well be different from the sample screenshots given in this book. Therefore, be flexible and adapt as necessary. The step-by-step procedures that follow, and the supporting screenshots, are based on eBay's UK site at the time of writing. The principles and basic processes will, however, not be much different from country to country, or from time to time.

REGISTER AS AN eBAY SELLER (FREE)

To sell on eBay you need to be a registered seller, and there's no charge for the registration itself. But once you start selling something, certain selling fees become payable to eBay. These selling fees – which are quite reasonable – vary from country to country and may also occasionally change. They are debited by eBay to your credit card or bank account only when you list and sell an item.

---

eBAY's SELLING FEES

Insertion Fee: This is the online equivalent of the fee you would pay to a newspaper or magazine for placing an advert in their publication. It is a non-refundable fee for listing the item for sale on eBay and it is charged to your account at the time you place your listing. The fee is according to the value of the item you're listing, and can start as low as a few pence/cents.

Optional extras: eBay also charges for certain additional options you might wish to choose in order to enhance your listing or to specify certain requirements. For example, you can include one photograph at no extra charge, but if you want several photos there will be a small charge for that (a few cents/pence each). If you want to set a reserve price, there's a small fee for that as well.

Final Value Fee: eBay charges an additional fee when the item is sold, based on the closing price at the end of that auction. If the item is not sold, this fee is not charged.

Other: There are several other fee variations too, depending on the kind of article, any bulk discounts offered to PowerSellers (sellers who consistently sell a significant volume of items and maintain a 98% feedback rating), and so on. Full details of the eBay selling fees are available on every country's eBay site via the Help menu.

The total cost of selling on eBay is therefore the **Insertion Fee**, plus any extras you've selected, added to the **Final Value Fee** as calculated for the particular item being auctioned. Because the Insertion Fee is payable upfront whether or not the item gets sold, it's advisable to prepare thoroughly before listing your item, so that you increase the likelihood of your item selling the first time you auction it. Otherwise you could be incurring a listing fee with no sale.

NOTE: HAVE YOUR CREDIT CARD AND BANK DETAILS AT HAND

You will be asked to provide details of your credit card or debit card and in some cases your bank account. This is to enable eBay to verify your existence as a 'real person' in order to minimize fraud and to protect the entire eBay community of buyers and sellers. The information is kept confidentially secured on eBay. There's no need to have any security concerns in this regard because eBay is a tried and trusted service that has been in existence since 1995.

---

1 **Sign in** on eBay if you're not already signed in.
2 Click on the **My eBay** tab (top right of the eBay page).
3 Browse down the left side of the My eBay window that opens, and under the heading **My Account**, click on **Personal Information** to open the **My eBay Account: Personal Information** page.

> ⸺ Sellers
> ▪ Categories
>
> **My Account**
> ▪ Personal Information
> ▪ Addresses
> ▪ Preferences
> ▪ Feedback
> ▪ Subscriptions
>
> **My Reviews & Guides**
>
> **Dispute Console**

4 At the bottom of that page, under the heading **Financial Information**, click on the **Edit** link beside the account (**Bank account** or the **Credit card** option) that you want your eBay selling fees charged to. You may be asked to sign in to your account again, as a security precaution.

Financial Information

If you are a seller, any eBay selling fees will be charged to your chosen account below. If you are a buyer, you can change how you pay for PayPal purchases through your PayPal account.

Bank account	Sort code: Not Specified	Edit
	Account number: Not Specified	
Credit card	Card number: Not Specified	Edit
	Expiry date: Not Specified	

You'll then be asked to create a seller account.

5 Click on the **Create a seller's account** link and in the window that opens follow the prompts to complete your account verification details. Be sure to enter the account name exactly as it is on your credit card or bank account statement.

Please create a seller account

Before you sell on eBay, you'll need to open a seller account for identification purposes.

Create a seller's account at no charge. It's fast and easy.

DO YOUR HOMEWORK BEFORE YOU LIST YOUR ITEM

Once you've completed your registration, you're ready to start creating your listing (the details of the item you wish to sell). To increase the likelihood of your item being sold the first time it's listed, you need to make sure it's attractive to would-be buyers. To get some ideas, simply browse eBay's completed listings to see how other sellers have listed items that are similar to yours and which they've already sold; then adapt your own listing accordingly.

1 On any eBay page click on the **Advanced Search** link.

2 In the **Search: Find Items** window that opens, type in a **keyword** of the item you want to sell, and use the ⌄ **down** arrow to select an appropriate **category** for that kind of item. (Type the keyword as singular rather than plural, as this will increase the number of items in the results list – e.g. type tricycle rather than tricycles.)

3 Be sure to click in the **check-box** against the words **Completed listings only**, to display only those items that have already had a successful sale.

4 Select any other **Sort** or **View** options from the headings below that.

5 When ready, click on the **Search** button.

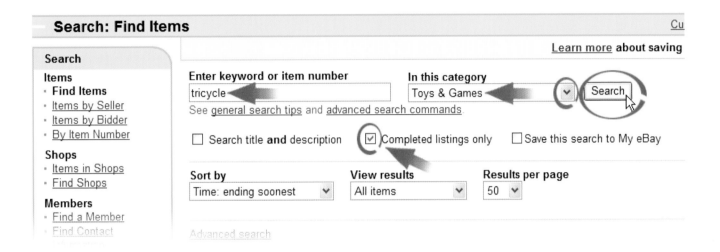

6 In the list that opens, click on the description of an item that is similar to what you're selling, to see more details.

7 In the details window that opens, study the various items in the list to get ideas for your own listing, and write these down:

– category; starting price

– whether to offer a fixed-price *Buy It Now* option

– description

– postage and packaging arrangements and costs

– payment options offered

– colour photograph angle, etc.

8 Click on any items and any links where you want to find out more details.

9 Scroll down an item's Web page to see more details, including the full description and a larger photo of the item.

10 Repeat the process with other similar items in the list to get a 'feel' of what would make your listing effective.

START THE LISTING PROCESS

1   Click on the **Sell** tab at the top of any eBay Web page to start the listing procedure.

Site Map

2   In the **List your item for sale** window that opens, type a brief name for your item – e.g. Girls Pink Tricycle. (This short name is simply for your own reference purposes and does not appear in the online listing as such.)

3   Click in the first radio button, next to **Quick Sell** (or **Keep it simple**, if that's what shows).

4   Click on the **Start selling** button to begin entering the details for your listing.

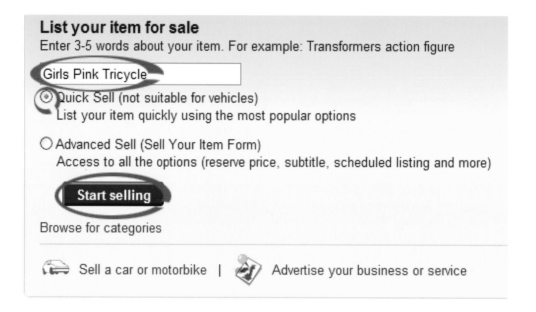

NOTE: THE EXTRA OPTIONS OF 'ADVANCED SELL'

A full list of the extra options available with **Advanced Sell** (versus **Quick Sell**) is available at: http://pages.ebay.co.uk/help/sell/selling-tools.html

---

Note that most of the eBay Web pages have links to additional topic-related help and tips pages to make it easy for you to follow the process with confidence.

ENTER EACH BLOCK OF DETAILS FOR YOUR LISTING

Armed with your research notes, start to enter all the details for your item.

Block 1 – Create a descriptive title for your item

Your item's title should help buyers find your item easily and quickly so that it sells first time round. Don't be vague in your title; for example, rather than entering just the words *girl's tricycle*, be more specific. And if something has more than one way of being described – e.g. trike and tricycle – include both terms to catch all the people who are searching for such an item. A good title is one that is an honest and accurate description of the item; a description that includes:

• the brand name, product name, size, colour, key specs if applicable, etc;

• whether it is new or used.

Try to make full and effective use of all or most of the 55 characters available for the title, and don't waste characters on meaningless words or exclamations such as 'great!', 'wow!', 'fantastic!' and so on.

Proofread your title very carefully; if you have any spelling errors, your item won't come up in eBay's search results and you will have missed the opportunity to sell to a potential buyer.

1 Give your item a good, accurate, descriptive **title** as per the guidelines above.

TIP: USE THE EBAY HELP LINKS

If you're not sure what something in the eBay forms means, click on the accompanying ⓐ link for additional information.

Block 2 – Select the category that best describes your item

Your item needs to be in a category in which people will search for that kind of item. If it's not, your prospective customers won't see it. Avoid resorting to using the vague *Other* category. Buyers who know what they want mostly search in the specific category for the item they're looking for and are unlikely to bother to check what's listed in *Other*. Choose the category that best describes the item you're selling. If you're uncertain, click the *Browse* categories tab to find a different category.

1 Choose the most appropriate **category**. eBay will offer a suggestion based on your descriptive title; but if their suggestion isn't suitable, for more options click on the **Browse categories** tab and select the category you think fits best.

2 Once you've clicked on the main category, another window opens for you to select a sub-category, and another, until to get to the most appropriate deepest-level **sub-category**.

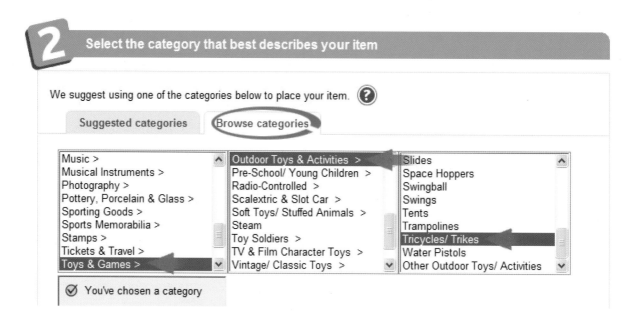

NOTE: EBAY CAN ADD EXTRA DETAILS FOR CERTAIN ITEMS

If you're selling an item such as a DVD, computer printer, or some other popular retail item, there is an option to have eBay automatically add extra details to your description, which may include a complimentary photo of your item (see screenshot below).

To get extra description details from eBay's data library:

1 Type the title/brand/model of the item you're selling and click on the **Search** button.

2 From the list of items eBay offers, click on the **OK** button of the item that matches what you're selling.

eBay can automatically fill your auction-style listing with information about your item.

EAN, Title or Leading Role

OK **Toy Story**
Annie Potts, Don Rickles, Jim Varney, John Morris, John Ratzenberger, Tim Allen, Tom Hanks
John Lasseter
UK:PG
EAN 8717418065713

Block 3 – Bring your item to life with pictures

Your photo (or photos) should give a clear and attractive view of the item you're selling so that the prospective buyer can see what s/he will be bidding on or buying now. Most sellers include a photo; if you don't, you'll definitely be at a disadvantage if there are several items like yours that buyers can choose from in the listings. You can upload one photo free of charge; for additional photos eBay charges a small fee. Depending on the value and complexity of your item, sometimes extra photos will help you get the sale.

> ### TIP: A GALLERY THUMBNAIL PHOTO
>
> In the framed box below the **Add a photo** buttons (see next screenshot), eBay gives you the option to include a small thumbnail version of your photo in the listings **Gallery** – that is, the list of similar items in a particular category. There is a small fee for this, but it is well worth clicking in the little check-box to select this option. Most other people will have these thumbnail photos next to their own items in the list. If you don't, buyers are likely to bypass your item and select one that does have a thumbnail photo to show them what the item looks like. eBay sometimes has sellers' specials whereby this and other options are free for a period of time.

1 If you haven't already done so, take digital photos of your item and save them to a folder that's easy to find on your computer.

2 Click on the **Add a photo** button to add an accompanying photo to your item's description.

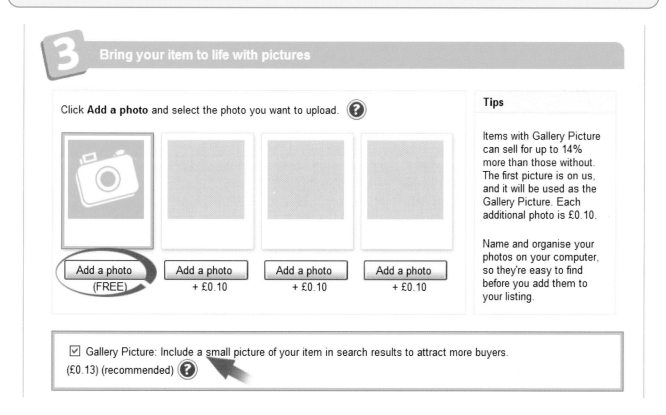

3 In the **Add a photo** dialogue box that opens (screenshot below left), click on the **Browse** button to find the digital photo where you've filed it on your computer.

4 In the **Choose File** box that opens (screenshot below center), browse to the folder that contains the photo you wish to upload, click on the **file name,** and click on **Open**. (The file name will now appear in the **Add a photo** dialogue box (screenshot below right).

5 In the **Add a photo** box, click on the **Upload photos** button.

Step 3 above

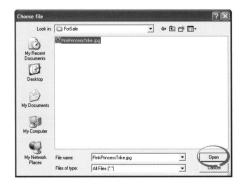

Step 4 above

Step 5 above

Block 4 – Describe the item you're selling

Here's your opportunity to describe all the features of the item you're selling. The description should be specific, useful and appealing. Notice that in the screenshot opposite, the seller states the reason for selling the item. Buyers like this kind of information because it can give them a better idea as to whether this is what they're looking for. For example, if someone is selling a document scanner, and their reason is that it is not compatible with Windows Vista, a buyer who has Windows XP on their computer might decide that this is just the item they need; after all, it's not being sold because it's faulty but simply because the seller no longer needs that particular model.

   In your detailed description always be sure to list those aspects that *you* would want to know if you were making the decision as a customer. That includes specifying any flaws, damage, etc. Be totally honest; if not, you could have a dissatisfied customer when s/he receives the item in the post. That, in turn, could lead to all sorts of hassles. Any payment methods other than PayPal, personal cheque or postal orders should be included in the item's description.

1 Fill in the **full description** you wish to have displayed in the final listing.

2 Use the **formatting buttons** above the description window to format any headings or to highlight any text in your description.

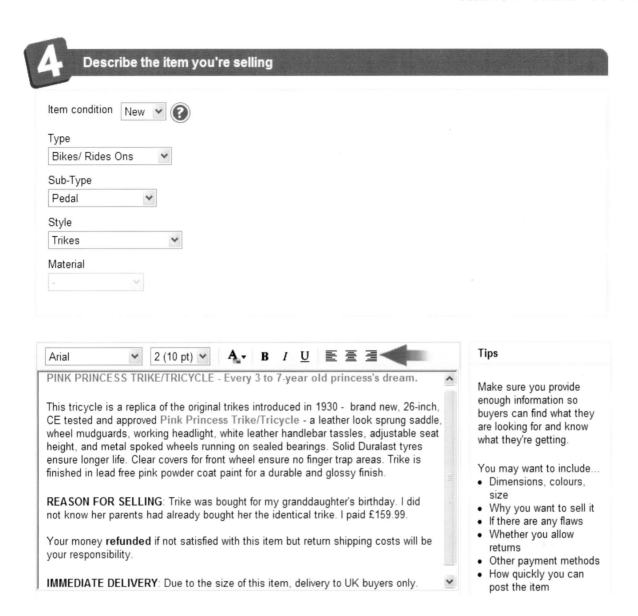

Block 5 – Set a price and also the postage & packaging details

Starting bid: Now it's time to make some key decisions regarding price, as well as the costs of postage and packaging (P&P) to the destinations to which you're prepared to ship the item once it's been sold. Remember, the starting price should be attractive to encourage bidding. It's a myth to believe that you need to set a high starting price so that you don't end up 'giving it away'. Experience has shown that a low starting price with no reserve actually encourages higher bids and higher final selling prices.

Reserve: If your item has a high value, you may want to consider setting a reserve price (lowest acceptable bid) for it. On lower-valued items a reserve can discourage bidders, especially if it is considered to be on the high side. So use this option with discretion. (There is an additional fee for selecting the Reserve option.)

Auction duration: There are five options to choose from. An auction can run for one, three, five, seven or ten days. If you set the duration at seven days, that would automatically include a weekend; this is useful for busy customers who rely on the weekends to see what's on offer so that they can be ready for the last-minute bidding near the end of the auction.

TIP: YOU CAN SCHEDULE A SPECIFIC START DATE AND TIME

For an extra fee, you can schedule your listing to start on a specific day and at a specific time, up to three weeks in advance. You can view pending items on your **My eBay** page, via the **Scheduled** link in the **All Selling** section.

Postal details: You need to decide whether you will sell the item internationally or just within your own country; and to which specific destinations you're prepared to ship it once it's sold. Be sure to specify this in your pricing details so that there are no misunderstandings later on. eBay offers a handy Postage Calculator that you can access via a link to calculate the postage charges to various destinations. Remember, international postage obviously costs more, so take this into account when setting your charges. And remember to add (and specify) any packaging costs too.

Returns policy: You should also spell out clearly what your returns policy is – under what circumstances you are prepared to accept the item back for a refund, and whether any returns fees will be deducted from the refund. For ideas on this, refer to other sellers' completed listings as explained on pages 52 and 53.

1 Enter your preferred starting bid price and use the ⌄ **down** arrow to select the auction **duration** you want.
2 Use the ⌄ **down** arrows to select the **postal destinations** and the kind of **service** you'll use, as well as the **postal cost** to each destination.
3 To **add more destinations or services**, click on the applicable link (see screenshot below).
4 Click on the **Postage Calculator** link for help with calculating postage costs.

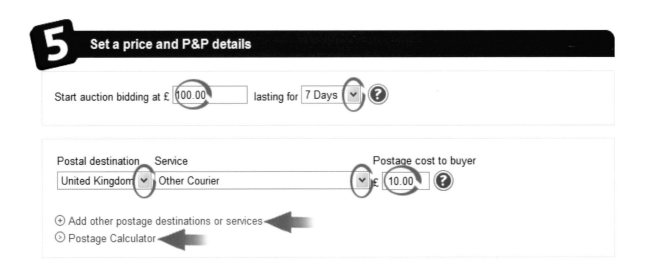

Block 6 – Decide how you'd like to be paid

This is an important aspect of your listing because the options you offer could affect whether or not a buyer is prepared or able to bid on or buy your item. For example, buyers prefer a safe and easy payment method, and PayPal certainly delivers that. So give your choice of payment method/s due consideration before you decide.

 YOUR PAYPAL E-MAIL ADDRESS When accepting <u>PayPal</u> as a payment method, be sure to enter your PayPal e-mail address, which may or may not be different from the address you used when you registered with eBay.

1 If you'll accept PayPal, click in the **check-box** and enter your **PayPal e-mail address**.

2 To add other payment options, click on the link **Show more payment options**.

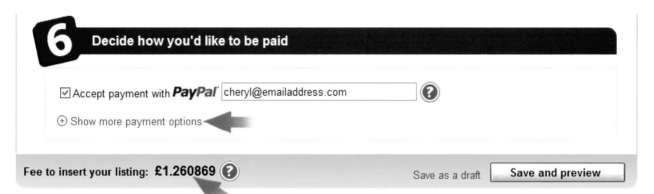

3 Click in the applicable check-boxes to select any other payment options you'll offer.

4 If necessary, go back to eBay Block 4 to provide details for payment options not offered in eBay's listing form.

Now that you've completed your listing process, eBay will display the estimated *Insertion Fee*. If your item sells, you'll be charged an additional *Final Value Fee* – a percentage of the final sale price.

To add the Reserve or *Buy It Now* options: Remember, at the start of this process we selected the *Quick Sell* (or *Keep it simple*) option. If we'd selected the *Advanced Sell* option, additional choices would have been displayed, including setting a *Reserve price* and a *Buy It Now* fixed price.

> **1** To view and use these additional options, click on the link **Sell Your Item form** (see bottom of next screenshot).

Saving and previewing your draft listing

> **1** To save your listing at any time and return at a later date to complete the details, click on the **Save as a draft** link at the bottom of the **Create Your Listing** page.
>
> **2** Once all the details have been entered, click on the **Save and preview** button to review your listing before you activate it. (You can still add or remove listing options and make changes even after clicking on the **Save and preview** button.)

Fee to insert your listing: **£1.260869** ?   Save as a draft   **Save and preview**

Any problems? Please contact Customer Support.

To view all listing options, switch to the Sell Your Item form now, and continue listing your item.

NOTE: A SAVED DRAFT CAN BE EDITED LATER

Once you click on the **Save as a draft** link or the **Save and preview** button, the next time you sign in and click on the **Sell** tab, your listing will be available and you can continue editing it. (Just click on the link that has the descriptive name you gave to your listing in Block 1.)

Sell

You're almost ready to sell this item. Please complete your listing.
New 26" Princess Pink Trike/Tricycle - girls ages 3 - 7 *
*Edited 17-Mar. Starting a new listing will delete this one.

 or

List vour item for sale

Check the details of your listing

After you click on the *Save and preview* button the following page will be displayed. Your total fees to this point are listed as well as a preview of what your advert will look like based on the selections you've previously made.

You'll be informed as to whether or not you need to verify your PayPal account if you intend to participate in global trade. (This is why it was important to verify your PayPal account when you signed up; to avoid the hassles of dealing with it at this listing point.)

Review your listing

The fee to insert your listing is **£1.260869**

Fees
Insertion fee:	£1.130434
Gallery fee:	£0.130435
Total: *	**£1.260869**

* Stated fees exclude VAT. Learn more about rounding and how VAT applies to you.

If your item sells, you will be charged a Final Value Fee, based on a percentage of the final sale price. Learn more about fees.

Your listing will be posted on the eBay site and can be viewed in My eBay. Your listing may not be immediately searchable by keyword or category for several hours, so eBay cannot guarantee exact listing duration in search results. The appearance of your listing in search results may be affected by listing format, end time, keywords, price, postage, Feedback, and Detailed Seller Ratings

---

 PROOFREAD EVERY DETAIL VERY CAREFULLY Once bidding has started, you cannot change the existing text of a listing (although you can add *extra* information to it – which is not always the ideal way to fix an error). So, be sure to check your item's details very carefully, including the title description. Having accurate and complete listing details will avoid complications arising later on.

---

1 Read through and check that your listing is as you want it. If it isn't, click on the **Edit listing** link to go back and make your revisions.

2 If you're happy with your listing, click on the **Continue** button. (You may be asked to re-enter your password again as you're now entering a secure page where you'll be asked to select your method of fee payments to eBay.)

Any problems? Please contact Customer Support.

TIP: SAVE YOUR LISTING AS A TEMPLATE

During the listing process eBay offers you the option to save your listing as a **template**. This means that when you want to sell your next item you don't need to re-type the shipping details, your preferred payment methods, font styles, etc. It's already in your pre-determined template.

CHOOSE HOW YOU WILL PAY YOUR eBAY FEES

There are several payment options, the availability of which may depend on your country.

eBAY SELLING FEES PAYMENT OPTIONS

eBay offers several options for paying the *Insertion* and *Final Item Value* seller's fees. Choose the one that best meets your needs and that can be used for your particular country.

PayPal: With this option the eBay invoice amount will be deducted automatically from your PayPal account each month and PayPal will collect the money from you according to your account arrangement with them.

Direct Debit: This option works only if your bank account is in the same country as the eBay website from which you're selling. Give eBay your bank or building society account number and bank sort code, and eBay will obtain the necessary authority from your bank or building society to debit your account with the amount of your monthly eBay invoice. (There will be a delay of roughly three weeks before this arrangement has been finalized.)

Credit Card: You can enter your Visa or MasterCard details in your eBay account for the payment of these fees, and eBay will debit your credit card account with the total of each month's invoice.

Cheque or Postal Order: You can mail a cheque or postal order to eBay if you live in the same country as the website you use for selling on eBay.

Changing your method: You can change your preferred payment method at any time via the **Account** section of your **My eBay** page.

Payment due date: Your invoice balance must be paid in full each month or your account may be suspended, in which case you could be responsible for any collection costs. The payment due date is either the 15th of the month or the last day of the month, depending on when eBay generates the invoice.

Trading Limit: If you don't have an automatic payment method on file (e.g. PayPal, credit card, bank debit order) there is a credit limit on your eBay account.

1 Click in the applicable **radio button** to make your selection.
2 Follow the instructions in the windows that open.

Pre-authorized Debit Payment option: This requires verification of your identity.

NOTE: VERIFICATION OF WHO YOU ARE

Bank account details: You may be asked to provide details of your local bank account as part of the verification process. eBay does not debit this account but uses the information solely for identification purposes.

Phone verification option: Note too that there may be an option to verify your identity via telephone; this will enable you to start selling immediately. With this option you enter your landline telephone number in the format indicated and select whether you want to receive the call immediately or in two minutes. You will then receive an automated call with a 4-digit verification number. Enter the 4-digit verification number on eBay and continue with your registration.

ACTIVATE YOUR ITEM'S LISTING

Once you're completely satisfied with every aspect of your listing's details, you're ready to list your item – either for immediate display on eBay's website or for display from a later date that you've scheduled (if you selected that option).

1   Click on the **List your item** button to list your item for sale at the eBay website.

| **List your item** | | Preview your listing | Edit listing

About eBay | Announcements | Security Centre | Policies | Site Map | Help

Copyright © 1995-2008 eBay Inc. All Rights Reserved. Designated trademarks and bra Agreement and Privacy Policy.

eBay official time

HANDLE QUESTIONS FROM PROSPECTIVE BUYERS PROMPTLY

You may well receive e-mail questions from prospective buyers about the item/s you have listed for auction or fixed-price sale. These are most likely 'hot' prospects who want to be sure that what you're offering is what they want. Or they may have some questions related to whether you're prepared to ship your item to a destination not mentioned in your listing. Attend to these queries promptly, with clear and complete answers. This will not only increase your chances of getting a good price, but if one of these prospects ends up buying your item you are more likely to get positive feedback ratings which will help you in any future sales or purchases.

eBay also has a feature where you can post questions and answers to your listing in order to minimize the number of e-mails you have to answer.

TIP: LEARN FROM THE QUESTIONS YOU RECEIVE

Sometimes a question – particularly if several people e-mail you with similar questions – can indicate that the information you have provided in your listing is not adequate. Take note; update your listing with this additional information, and make sure that any items you sell in the future include that kind of information. In this way you can continue to hone your listing skills each time you offer something on eBay.

MONITORING YOUR ITEMS IN *My eBay*

Your *My eBay* section (accessible from the tab at the top right of any eBay page) makes it easy to keep track of all your buying and selling activities. This is particularly helpful when you have several listings going on at the same time. Click on the applicable links in *My eBay* to see the details.

My eBay

My eBay Views

My Summary

All Buying ◄
- Watching (13)
- Bidding
- Bid Assistant
- Best Offers
- Won (7)
- Didn't Win (2)

All Selling ◄
- Scheduled
- Selling
- Sold
- Unsold (1) ◄
Marketing Tools

Want It Now

My Messages (3)

All Favourites
- Searches
- Sellers

TIP: YOU CAN RE-LIST ANY UNSOLD ITEM – FOR FREE

The **Unsold** category contains any items that did not sell by the end of your auction period. You can click on this link to re-list such items in a new auction or *Buy It Now* offering. Use any e-mail queries you received to help you find any factors that may have resulted in the no-sale, and improve your new listing if necessary – including, perhaps, lowering your starting price.

ONCE YOUR ITEM IS SOLD

Once your successful listing period has ended (after one, three, five, seven or ten days, as specified by you when you created your listing), eBay will send an e-mail to both you and your successful buyer with all the final details of the transaction, including payment instructions. If you selected PayPal as the payment method, you'll be advised by PayPal as soon as payment has been received.

1   If necessary, **contact your buyer** immediately to finalize payment and delivery arrangements.

2   If payment is via PayPal, you'll receive a **You've got cash** e-mail. Click on the e-mail to **log in** at PayPal and view the details of the payment.

3   Once you're happy that full payment has been received as per your listing details, **dispatch the item** to its new owner **without delay** and advise your customer of the shipping details (date, method, any post office tracking number, etc.).

4   **Leave feedback** for your customer and invite them to do the same for you.

That's it! You've completed a successful sale at the world's largest online auction website.

LEARNING MORE ABOUT eBAY

eBay offers lots of other facilities and assistance – too many to include in this starter book for absolute beginners. As you gain experience with the basics of buying and selling on eBay you can explore many of the Help links and various aspects of this huge marketplace on the Web. To help you in this regard, here are a few useful pointers:

Find information on eBay:

• Click on the Site Map link below the tabs at the top right of any eBay page and explore links that look interesting to you.

Use the Help menu:

• Mouse over the **Help** tab at the top right of any eBay page and click on a menu item that looks relevant to what you need help on.

Use the eBay Glossary of Terms:

• If you're not sure what a particular term means, click on the **Help** tab, type **eBay glossary** in the Help search window and click on the **Search Help Pages** button.

Learn how to deal with buyer or seller non-performance:

• Do a Help search on the keyword **non-performance** (and any other similar terms) to learn how to deal with a situation where a buyer or a seller does not perform as agreed.

NEXT: OTHER OPTIONS AND OTHER AUCTION SITES

As we've seen, eBay is not always the easiest buying or selling option for every country in the world. So, in the next chapter you'll see how to find other useful alternatives, including using local auctions websites as well as buying and selling via straightforward online classified adverts.

5 Exploring other options

TRADING AT LOCALLY DEVELOPED AUCTION SITES

Many online buyers and sellers like to use auction websites developed and managed in their own countries. For some it's simply a matter of national loyalty or pride. For others, it's for practical reasons.

SOME ADVANTAGES OF TRADING LOCALLY

There are a number of definite advantages to using locally developed and managed websites for trading at online auctions or buying at online stores. Here are some:

- **Same-currency benefits:** Both the buyer and the seller are trading in the same currency. This is both convenient and also cost-effective:
  - No foreign exchange is involved, so there are no associated exchange rate fluctuation risks or the added cost of foreign exchange bank commissions.
  - Fast and secure payments through local Internet banking.

- **PayPal's country limitations are not an issue:** One important need that sellers have is the ability to receive or at least transfer buyers' payments into their bank account in their own country. PayPal's inability to meet this need in a number of countries (South Africa, Sri Lanka and Bermuda being just three examples) effectively makes it impossible for sellers to sell items from these countries at offshore auction sites like eBay. (Not everyone has the facility of an offshore bank account.) Therefore, if you are one of those many sellers who have problems using PayPal to receive funds, then a local online auction site would be a viable alternative. For example, in South Africa there's an excellent and reputable online auctions site at **www.bidorbuy.co.za** which offers the option to bid on something or buy it outright, much like eBay. And New Zealand has its **www.trademe.co.nz** auctions site. Some local online auction websites even have their own local equivalent of eBay's PayPal – for example, the bobPay service of bidorbuy.co.za and the Pay Now service of trademe.co.nz – that cater for local currency and local banking arrangements.

- **Some local sites have locally-tuned policies:** For example, bidorbuy.co.za does not charge an upfront selling (listing) fee; you pay only when the item is sold. And trademe.co.nz doesn't even charge a listing fee for basic listings.

- **Lower shipping costs:** In-country shipping/postage costs are usually much lower than for international transactions.

- **Less selling competition:** Being a smaller online environment compared with huge international sites, local sites usually have far less competition for sellers who wish to set up a profitable online business.

- **Same-city trades have even more benefits:**
  - *See what you're buying:* If the buyer and seller are in the same city, the buyer can often see the item physically before making the commitment to buy – obviously not possible with international purchases.
  - *Face-to-face goods/cash exchange:* The buyer and seller can meet in person to do the exchange (item for cash), thereby limiting any potential risks.
  - *Virtually no delivery costs:* You only pay for your own transport cost of getting to the hand-over rendezvous. You don't, therefore, incur any postage costs.
  - *Immediate delivery/collection:* There's no delay in terms of mailing, waiting for funds to be confirmed, and so on. It's also ideal when large items such as boats or motor vehicles are being traded.

Finding local online auction websites

Whatever one's reason for considering local websites, it's fun and also interesting to shop around and see what's available locally. Use a search engine to find out if your country has any good local auction sites:

1 Do a search for **online auctions+your country** (e.g. **online auctions+peru, online auctions+anguilla**).

Alternatively:

2 Search for: **online auctions directory+your country**.

Here's one site you might want to check for auction sites in your own country. It lists auction sites worldwide: **www.world-online-auctions.com**

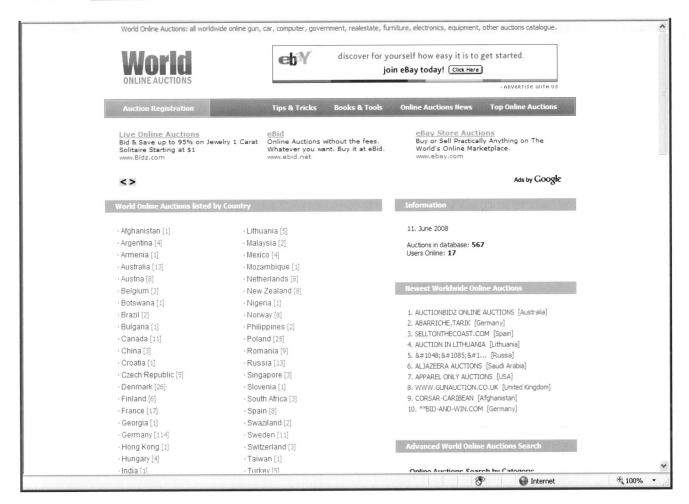

Here are two examples of local websites site that such a search can discover:

Example of an excellent locally developed and managed online auction site (in South Africa) – bidorbuy.co.za

Example of another locally developed and managed online auction site – in New Zealand – trademe.co.nz

ONLINE CLASSIFIED ADS

Another option besides auction sites is buying or selling via online classified advertisements. One very popular website that offers online classifieds is craigslist.

CRAIGSLIST

One of the world's most widely used websites for local online trading is called *craigslist.org*, an online site for city-specific classified ads and forums, with coverage approaching 500 cities worldwide. At craigslist you can buy or sell/advertise everything from merchandise, real estate and various services, to garage sales, employment opportunities and more. To put craigslist into perspective, here are some interesting statistics given on the craigslist website (It is possible that information on websites is not always updated regularly):

- The site attracts 9 billion page-views per day, as per Alexa ('The Web Information Company').
- It is currently ranked number 7 in page-views worldwide, above the BBC, Disney and Amazon.
- The companies higher up in the Alexa rankings have a large number of employees each – from Yahoo's and Google's 10,000 each, to eBay's 12,000 and Time Warner's 90,000. craigslist has 23 employees.

HOW TO BUY FROM CRAIGSLIST

1   Go to **www.craigslist.org** and a simple Web page will open, listing the countries and cities in which you'll find a craigslist classifieds listing.

craigslist	us cities	united states		canada	asia	europe	int'l cities
	atlanta	alabama	missouri	alberta	bangladesh	austria	amsterdam
help pages	austin	alaska	montana	brit columbia	china	belgium	athens
login	boston	arizona	nebraska	manitoba	india	czech repub	bangalore
	chicago	arkansas	nevada	n brunswick	indonesia	denmark	bangkok
factsheet	dallas	california	n hampshire	newf & lab	israel	finland	beijing
avoid scams	denver	colorado	new jersey	nova scotia	japan	france	barcelona
	detroit	connecticut	new mexico	ontario	korea	germany	berlin
your safety	honolulu	delaware	new york	pei	lebanon	great britain	buenos aires
best-ofs	houston	dc	n carolina	quebec	malaysia	greece	delhi
	las vegas	florida	north dakota	saskatchwn	pakistan	hungary	dublin
job boards	los angeles	georgia	ohio	ca cities	philippines	ireland	hong kong
movie	miami	guam	oklahoma	calgary	singapore	italy	london
minneapolis	hawaii	oregon	edmonton	taiwan	netherlands	madrid

The home page at www.craigslist.org

2 Click on your **country** and then a **city** (or directly on a city's name if it's listed on that home page) and you'll arrive at that city's classified ads list.

3 In the **search craigslist** window enter the **keyword(s)** (singular rather than plural) to describe what item you're looking for and choose the applicable **classification** from the drop-down menu.

4 Click on the ▷ **search** button to start the search.

craigslist > **united kingdom** ▾

choose the site nearest you (or suggest a new one):

aberdeen
belfast
birmingham
brighton
bristol
cambridge, UK
cardiff / wales

If your city isn't listed, you can click on the link **(or suggest a new one)** to enter the forum and make your request.

---

craigslist uk

london ▾

post to classifieds

my account

help, faq, abuse, legal

search craigslist

photo printer

for sale ▾ ▷

community
events
gigs
houses
jobs
personals
job wanted
for sale
services

31 1 2 3 4 5 6

avoid scams & fraud

personal safety tips

craigslist factsheet

best-of-craigslist

job boards compared

craigslist movie & dvd

community

artists	activities
classes	childcare
events	local news
general	lost+found
groups	musicians
pets	rideshare
politics	volunteers

personals

strictly platonic
women seek women
women seeking men
men seeking women
men seeking men
misc romance
casual encounters
missed connections
rants and raves

discussion forums

apple	haiku	philos
arts	health	politic
atheist	help	psych
autos	history	queer
beauty	houses	recover
bikes	jobs	religion
celebs	jokes	rofo
comp	knit	science

houses

flats/houses
holiday rentals
house swap
house wanted
office / commercial
parking / storage
property for sale
rooms / shared
sublets / temporary

for sale

barter	arts+crafts
bikes	auto parts
boats	baby+kids
books	boot/rummage
business	cars+vans
caravans	cds/dvd/vhs
computer	clothes+acc
free	collectables
garden	electronics
general	furniture
material	games+toys
sporting	household
tickets	jewellery
tools	motorcycles
wanted	music instr
	photo+video

jobs

accounting+finance
admin / office
arch / engineering
art / media / design
biotech / science
business / mgmt
customer service
education
food / drink / hosp
general labour
government
human resources
internet engineers
legal / paralegal
manufacturing
marketing / pr / ad
medical / health
property
retail / wholesale
sales / biz dev
salon / spa / fitness
security
skilled trade / craft
software / qa / dba
systems / network
technical support
third sector

UK	countries
aberdeen	argentina
belfast	australia
birmingham	austria
brighton	bangladesh
bristol	belgium
cambridge	brazil
cardiff / wales	canada
devon / cornwall	caribbean
east anglia	chile
east midlands	china
edinburgh	colombia
glasgow	costa rica
hampshire	czech repub
leeds	denmark
liverpool	egypt
london	finland
manchester	france
newcastle	germany
oxford	great britain
sheffield	greece
	hungary
US/CA	india
boston	indonesia
chicago	ireland
los angeles	israel
miami	italy
montreal	japan
new york	korea
seattle	lebanon
sf bayarea	malaysia
toronto	mexico
vancouver	micronesia
wash dc	netherlands
	new zealand
intl	norway
amsterdam	pakistan
bangalore	panama

5 In the search results page that opens, click on the item that interests you. You can also click on the text **pic** – where available – to see a photo of the item; see example below.

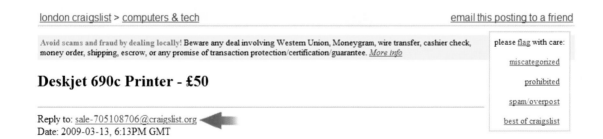

london craigslist > for sale / wanted

search for: photo printer   in: all for sale / wanted ▾   Search   ☐ only search titles

price: min   max   ☐ has image

<< Prev   **Found: 5 Displaying: 1 - 5**

Mar 13 - Deskjet 690c Printer - £50 - (North London) pic <<*computers & tech*

Mar 12 - Free Printers - (London W9) <<*computers & tech*

Feb 27 - HP Deskjet F380 - £30 - (London) pic <<*computers & tech*

Feb 16 - Dell Dimension PC - Epson Scanner & Printer £150 - (Chelsea) pic <<*computers & tech*

Feb 6 - Epson Stylus Photo £15 - pic <<*computers & tech*

<< Prev   **Found: 5 Displaying: 1 - 5**

6 In the listing's detailed view, click on the **Reply to**: e-mail address displayed to request more information or to discuss a possible purchase with the seller.

7 When your e-mail client opens, type your e-mail and send it to that address.

london craigslist > computers & tech   email this posting to a friend

Avoid scams and fraud by dealing locally! Beware any deal involving Western Union, Moneygram, wire transfer, cashier check, money order, shipping, escrow, or any promise of transaction protection/certification/guarantee. *More info*

please flag with care:

miscategorized

prohibited

spam/overpost

best of craigslist

Deskjet 690c Printer - £50

Reply to: sale-705108706@craigslist.org ◀
Date: 2009-03-13, 6:13PM GMT

HP Deskjet 690c
600 x 600 dots per inch 600 x 300 for color. Print up to five pages per minute for black text and up to 1.7 pages-per-minute in color.
You can print on cardstock, envelopes, labels, transparencies and even iron-on transfers. A continuous feed feature also lets you print banners.

£50.00
cash only

Location: North London ., CA
it's NOT ok to contact this poster with services or other commercial interests

PostingID: 705108706

NOTE: E-MAILS ARE ROUTED VIA CRAIGSLIST

Notice the number in the e-mail address – <u>sale-705108706@craigslist.org</u>. That number is the *PostingID* reference number that appears in the advert. Your e-mail will not go directly to the seller, but via craigslist who will then forward it on to the seller (with that *PostingID*) on your behalf. This protects the seller's e-mail address. Should the seller decide that you seem to be the best prospective buyer, and therefore wishes to respond to you, s/he will send you an e-mail. You can then communicate directly with each another about the item, and also arrange where and when the pickup or delivery of the item will take place.

HOW TO SELL USING CRAIGSLIST

1 In the left-hand column of links, click on **post to classifieds**.

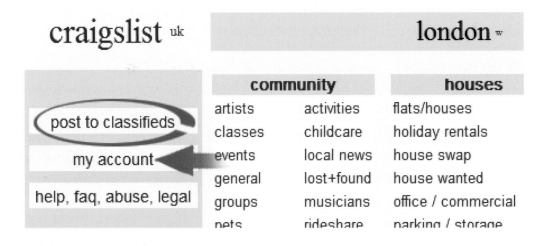

TIP: SAVE TIME BY OPENING A USER ACCOUNT

Although it is not entirely necessary to register a User Account at craigslist.org, if you're planning to do a lot of buying and selling via its classifieds, having an account would save you time by not having to re-enter your personal data each time. Simply click on **My Account** (screenshot above) and follow the prompts.

2 Whether or not you register, follow the craigslist prompts to select a suitable category.
3 In the posting form that opens, enter the necessary details and click on the options you require.
4 When done, click on **Continue**.

NOTE: MENU LIST

You can move around in craigslist via the other menu items in the left-hand column of the home page or any other page. It's pretty straightforward.

TIPS FOR BUYING OR SELLING ON CRAIGSLIST

1 Face-to-face trading: Because the listings are city-based, if the item advertised is in your city, you can do the transaction face to face. This means that if you're the buyer, you can see the item for yourself. If you're the seller, you can get paid there and then, in cash, before you hand the item over to the buyer.

2 Choose a safe place to meet: Don't invite buyers or sellers to your home. Rather arrange to meet at a safe public place like a café, coffee house or the like.

3 Tell a friend: Let a friend or family member know where you're going and how long you expect to be – just in case. Better still, ask someone to go with you.

4 Take a cell phone with you: If you have a cell phone, it's a good idea to take it with you in case you need to call someone for whatever reason.

5 Trust your instincts: Unfortunately we live in a world of con-artists and criminals. So trust your instincts. If something feels shady or risky, cancel the deal and go/stay home.

6 Don't 'buy into' any delaying tactics: If you're selling, don't part with your item until you feel the money in your hand. Don't accept any stories that the buyer will take the item and get the money from the car, or the ATM. That could be the last time you see your item and you may have to return home empty-handed with no item and no money.

LEARNING MORE ABOUT ONLINE BUYING AND SELLING

You should now be pretty competent at buying and selling online. Yet there's never really an end to learning about what else can be done. We suggest you make frequent use of the Help menus on all websites and explore the links to any tutorials and additional information. Another good place to pick up useful insights and tips is by visiting the discussion forums at the websites themselves, or at independent websites and web logs (blogs). You can search for useful sites by using keywords such as: online auction tips, online auction insights, online auction blogs and online auction forums.

Many people actually make a handsome living by selling at their own eBay store, or at the Amazon marketplace. So, there are lots of opportunities ahead if you're interested in pursuing them.

We wish you much success.

All the best!

My website log-in details

Website	My User Name	My Password	E-mail Address I Used

Our thanks to

Becky and Jake Chalmers
for their eBay input

Heidi Smith
for her craigslist input

and our acknowledgements and thanks to

the various online buying and selling and related websites
we have had the opportunity to promote by means of
this educational publication:

www.AlertPay.com

www.amazon.com

www.bidorbuy.co.za

www.craigslist.org

www.ebay.com

www.PayPal.com

www.trademe.co.za

Other useful websites mentioned in this book

www.world-online-auctions.com
world online auctions listed by country

www.wikipedia.com
free online encyclopaedia

www.about.com
free online info and advice

www.ReallyEasyComputerBooks.com
Cheryl's and Gavin's home site for our
Really, Really, Really Easy Computer Books

INDEX

NEW
HOLLAND

First published in 2009 by New Holland Publishers (UK) Ltd
London · Cape Town · Sydney · Auckland

Garfield House
86–88 Edgware Road
London, W2 2EA
United Kingdom
www.newhollandpublishers.com

80 McKenzie Street
Cape Town 8001
South Africa

Unit 1, 66 Gibbes Street
Chatswood, NSW 2067
Australia

218 Lake Road
Northcote, Auckland
New Zealand

10 9 8 7 6 5 4 3 2 1
ISBN 978 1 84773 074 9

Editor: Amy Corstorphine
Design: AG&G Books
Production: Laurence Poos
DTP: Peter Gwyer
Editorial Direction: Rosemary Wilkinson

Printed and bound by Times Offset, Malaysia

Credits